THE GREAT TEMPLES

OF

INDIA, CEYLON, AND BURMA

THE GREAT TEMPLES

OF

INDIA, CEYLON, AND BURMA

RAJENDRA LALA

GYAN

Published by

Gyan Publishing House
5, Ansari Road
Daryaganj, New Delhi-110002
Phone: 011-47034999, 9811692060
E-mail: books@gyanbooks.com

Distribution Network
gyanbooks.com
India, USA, Canada, UK, Australia

ISBN: 978-93-6920-017-7 (PB)

First Published, 1898

2nd Impression 2025

Printed at: Gyan Press, Delhi.

THE GREAT TEMPLES OF INDIA, CEYLON, AND BURMA
Author: RAJENDRA LALA

TEMPLE OF JAGANNATH, PURI.

THE GREAT TEMPLES

OF

INDIA, CEYLON, AND BURMA.

COMPILED FROM WILLIAMS, HUNTER, WILKINS, RAJENDRA LALA MITRA, AND OTHER WRITERS.

1898.

CONTENTS.

THE GREAT TEMPLES

OF

INDIA, CEYLON, AND BURMA.

INTRODUCTION.

INDIA has been called the "Land of Temples" in consequence of their number. In Ceylon and Burma, in addition to temples, there are semicircular or conical buildings, called *dagabas*, supposed to contain relics of Buddha. Considering the vast number of erections of both kinds, only a few of the principal can be described. The accounts will be classified under four heads—HINDU, SIKH, JAIN, and BUDDHIST. Buildings of the first three classes are mainly found in India; those of the fourth class in Ceylon and Burma. The arrangement followed will be chiefly geographical.

I. HINDU TEMPLES.

KALIGHAT.

A commencement is made with this temple, not on account of its importance, but from its position in the capital of the country.

CALCUTTA derives its name from Kali-ghat, the shrine of the goddess Kali, close to the old course of the Ganges, or Adi-Ganga, about a mile to the south of the Calcutta outskirts. The neighbouring country was known, in very remote times, as *Kali-kshetra*, the field of Kali. The Adi-Ganga is still venerated as the ancient channel by which the Ganges poured her waters towards the ocean, before they were diverted into the present Hugli. This old course, in many parts now little more than a series is depressions and shallow pools, is marked by shrines and burning *ghats* for the dead. The present temple is about 300 years old, and has no pretensions to beauty or grandeur.

Kali is often simply called Devi, 'the goddess' or Mahadevi. She is said to be the wife of Siva and daughter of Himavat, the Himalaya mountains. She has two characters, one mild, the other fierce; it is under the latter that she is specially worshipped. In her milder form she is Uma, 'light,' Parvati, 'the mountaineer.' In her terrible form she is Durga, 'the inaccessible'; Kali, 'the black'; Chandika, 'the fierce'; and Bhairavi, 'the terrible.'

Kali is represented as a black or dark-blue woman with 4 arms. In one hand she has a sword, in another the head of the giant she has slain, with the two others she is encouraging her worshippers. For earrings she has two dead bodies; she wears a necklace of skulls; her only clothing is a girdle made of dead men's hands, and her tongue protrudes from her mouth. Her eyes are red as those of a drunkard, and her breasts are besmeared with blood. She stands with one foot on the thigh, and the other on the breast of her husband. After her victory over the giant, she danced for joy so furiously that the earth trembled beneath her weight. At the request of the gods, Siva asked her to stop; but as, owing to her excitement, she did not notice him, he lay down among the slain. She continued dancing until she caught sight of her husband under her feet; upon which she thrust out her tongue.

The KALIKA PURANA gives an account of the offerings which are pleasing to the goddess. Siva, addressing his sons, the Bhairavas, says:

"The flesh of the antelope and the rhinoceros give my beloved delight for 500 years. By a human sacrifice, attended by the forms laid down, Devi is pleased a thousand years; and by the sacrifice of 3 men, a lakh of years. By human flesh Kamakhya, Chandika, and Bhairava, who assume my shape, are pleased a thousand years. An oblation of blood which has been rendered pure by holy texts, is equal to ambrosia; the head and flesh also afford much delight to Chandika. Blood drawn from the offerer's own body is looked upon as a proper oblation to the goddess Chandika.

KALI DANCING.

"Let the sacrificer repeat the word Kali twice, and say, 'Hail, Devi! goddess of thunder; hail, iron-sceptred goddess!' Let him then take the axe in his hand, and again invoke the same by the Kalaratri text, as follows: 'Let the sacrificer say, Hrang, Hrang! Kali, Kali! O horrid-toothed goddess! Eat, cut, destroy all the malignant; cut with thy axe; bind, bind; seize, seize; drink blood! Spheng, spheng! secure, secure, Salutation to Kali.' The axe being invoked by this text, called the Kalaratri Mantra, Kalaratri herself presides over the axe, uplifted for the sacrificer's enemies.

"An enemy may be immolated by proxy, substituting a buffalo or a goat, and calling the victim by the name of the enemy through the whole ceremony, thereby infusing, by holy texts, the soul of the enemy into the body of the victim; which will when immolated deprive the foe of life also. On this occasion let the sacrificer say: 'O goddess of horrid forms! O Chandika! Eat, devour such an one my enemy. Consort of fire, salutation to fire. This is the enemy who has done me mischief now personated by an animal—destroy him, O Mahamari!'"

The Thugs, who used to murder and rob unsuspecting travellers, made offerings to Kali before they set out, and expected her to preserve them from detection.

Supposed Origin of the Temple.—Parvati destroyed herself at the slight shown to her husband by her father Daksha, who had not invited him to the sacrifice. Siva was inconsolable at her loss, and throwing her corpse over his shoulder, wandered through the earth, causing the greatest consternation and trouble. Vishnu, appealed to by mankind in their distress, let his discus fly through the air, by which Parvati's body was cut into fifty parts, and wherever any part touched the ground a temple rose. It is said that at Kali Ghat the second toe of her left foot is preserved.

Sacrifices.—To this temple at Kali Ghat pilgrims come every day in the year, but on the days of any festival connected with the worship of Siva or Durga, immense crowds assemble. The object of the pilgrims is not simply to walk round the building, and try to catch a glimpse of her black face as they pass in front of the image, but to sacrifice a kid, sheep, or buffalo. Parents desirous of sons, families in any great sorrow vow to Kali that if a son be given, or the trouble that oppresses them be removed, a kid will be sacrificed to her.

This temple is a source of considerable profit to the proprietors, as not only do the pilgrims make their offerings, but a fee of 4 annas is taken for every kid that is sacrificed there; and on some days the victims are numbered by hundreds, if not by thousands. The Haldar family divide the proceeds among themselves. Each receives the offerings for a week or ten days; but on the great festival days all attend and divide the receipts amongst them.

The court yard of the temple looks like a slaughter house, while the smell is sickening. On busy days there is a noisy bustling crowd, each one trying to get his gift first attended to.

The people bring their victims, pay the fee, and the priest puts a little vermilion on each head. When their turn comes, the executioner takes the animal, fixes its head in the frame, and then beheads it. A little of the blood is placed in front of the idol, and the pilgrim takes away the headless body.

ORISSA TEMPLES.

The province of ORISSA lies to the south-west of Bengal along the coast, from a little beyond the mouth of the Subanrekha to the Chilka Lake. The area is 24,000 miles—about the size of Oudh, but the population is only about 5 millions. A great part of the interior consists of rugged hills, covered with jungle, and infested by wild beasts.

The name is derived from *Odradesa*, the country of the *Odras*. In ancient times it was called UTKALA.

The Uriyas, who inhabit the coast, speak a language very like Bengali. The province has been greatly neglected. In some inland parts a cart is nearly as great a novelty as a balloon. The people are in general, ignorant, apathetic and superstitious ; but there is a gradual improvement.

Although thus backward, Orissa has been, for many centuries, the Holy Land of the Hindus. From the moment the pilgrim passes the Baitarani river, he treads on holy ground ; before him is the promised land, which he has been taught to regard as a place of preparation for heaven. The three principal temples are at PURI and KONARAK on the coast, and BHUVANESWARA, inland, which will be described in turn. The hills contain several cave temples, but they are much inferior to some in other parts of India.

THE TEMPLE OF JAGANNATH AT PURI.

PURI is situated on the coast, separated from the sea by low sandy ridges. The streets are mean and narrow, with the exception of the principal avenue which leads from the temple to the country house of Jagannath. The population is about 24,000.

The most ancient name of the place was *Nilachila*, 'blue hill,' given to it to ennoble one of the sand ridges in the centre of the town, barely 20 feet high, on which the temple now stands. For centuries past, the city has been looked upon as the holiest on the face of the earth, and it is pre-eminently PURI, THE CITY.

The early history of Puri is very doubtful. It is certain however that from about 400 B.C. to 200 A.D., Orissa was mainly Buddhist. This is proved by the rock-cut edicts in Orissa of Asoka, the famous Buddhist king. The legend is that Khema, one of the disciples of Buddha, took a tooth from the funeral pile of Buddha, and gave it to Brahmadatta, king of Kalinga, who built a magnificent temple for its reception. The place where it was kept was called *Dantapura*, 'the city of the tooth.' About 300 A.D. the king of Kalinga was in sore trouble from his enemies. To save the tooth, he told his daughter to hide it in her hair and take it to Ceylon. There it was received with great honour, and placed in a splendid temple.

The change from Buddhism to Hinduism was gradual. The Brahmans persuaded the people that he whom they called Buddha was no other than Vishnu ; and that kindness to all living beings was one of his commands.

The present temple is said to have been built by Raja Anangabhima Deva. He ruled all the country from the Hugli to the Godavari. Unhappily he killed a Brahman, and the rest of his life was spent in endeavouring to expirate his guilt. It is said that he bridged 10 broad rivers, constructed 152 *ghats*, and countless other public works. Among the temples which he built was the shrine of Jagannath. Gold and jewels to the value of 15 lakhs of measures of gold were set apart for the work. For 14 years the artificers laboured, and the temple was finished in 1198 A.D.

The Temple.—The enclosure is nearly in the form of a square, 652 feet long, and 644 broad. The interior is protected by a massive stone wall, 22 feet high. Within rise numerous temples, dedicated to the various forms in which the god is imagined, &c. The great pagoda is the one dedicated to Jagannath. Its conical tower, elaborately carved, rises 192 feet high, black with time and surmounted by the wheel and flag of Vishnu. Outside the principal entrance, called the Lion Gate, in the square where the pilgrims chiefly throng, is a beautiful pillar of a single stone, which stood for centuries before the temple of the Sun at Konarak, 20 miles up the coast. The temple of Jagannath consists of 4 chambers, communicating with each other, *viz.*, the Hall of Offerings; the Pillared Hall for the musicians and dancing girls; the Hall of Audience; and lastly the Sanctuary itself, containing rude images of Jagannath, his brother Balabhadra, and his sister Subhadra.

The following is one legend with regard to the origin of the image. When Krishna was shot, his bones were left lying under the tree till some pious person placed them in a box. Raja Indradyumna was directed to form an image, and place in it their bones. The king prayed to Visvakarma, to assist him in making the image. The artificer of the gods promised to do so on condition that he was not disturbed. Though the king consented, after 15 days he tried to see Visvakarma at work, but there was only an ugly image without hands or feet.

The image of Jagannath has circular eyes, a straight head line, a square knob on the top, and black colour. The nose is large and hooked. The mouth is crescent-shaped. The height is 84 yavas, barley-corns or finger-breadths—about 6 feet.

The image of Balabhadra resembles that of Jagannath, but differs in some respects. The eyes are oval and placed slantingly; the mouth is indicated by paint in the form of a crescent. The nose is large and very much hooked. The nostrils are indicated by two red spots. There is no carving or painting of any kind to indicate the ears. The head is divided into two curves, projecting forward. On the crown of the head there is a rounded knob. Seen sideways, the face has a nearly straight line, with two hooked projections. The arms project in a line with the mouth, ending in stumps without any hands. The body is carved out of one block of wood, and the arms and forearms are nailed to it. The image is painted white. The height is 85 yavas.

BALABHADRA.

SUBHADRA.

The image of Subhadra is of a yellow colour, and has a rounded head. The eyes are oval, and the nose is not quite as much curved as that of the preceding two. The height is 54 yavas.

Dr. Rajendralala Mitra says that the images "are exceedingly ugly, and the most hideous caricatures of the human face divine."*

The images are placed on a stone platform, 4 feet high and 16 feet long. Jagannath is to the left, Subhadra in the middle, and Balabhadra to the right.

The images have several dresses each day. The first at dawn is the simplest. Then comes the leisure hour dress in which the divinities pass a good deal of the morning. It is replaced by the afternoon dress. The next is that which they put on when they smear themselves with sandal-paste. The most important is the court dress which is put on soon after dusk, immediately after the evening meal.

* *Antiquities of Orissa*, Vol. ii., pp. 123. The engravings are copied exactly from the drawings in this standard authority. The whole account of the temples in Orissa is chiefly taken from the same work.

Pilgrims in the Audience Hall, standing in front of a bar of sandal-wood, behold the lord of the world in the sanctuary in front. Persons paying largely are allowed to cross the bar and enter the sanctuary. The sanctuary is so dark that, without the aid of a lamp, nothing is visible within it even at midday.

JAGANNATH DRESSED.

Mahaprasad or Sacred Food.—The priests impress upon the pilgrims the impropriety of dressing food within the holy city, and the temple kitchen thus secures the monopoly of cooking for the multitude. The cooks employed are of the lowest caste, but after the food is offered to the divinity, it is called *Mahaprasad*, and esteemed the holiest of the holy in the universe, and the highest gods are blessed if they can partake of it. A single particle of it is sufficient to wash off the moral taint of the greatest crimes that created beings can commit. The murder of parents, spiritual guides, Brahmans, the slaughter of cows, the theft of gold and of divine images, all become innocuous the moment the guilty person reverently puts a grain of the *Mahaprasad* on his tongue. On the other hand, there is no crime so heinous as that of treating it disrespectfully.

It should be eaten the moment it is got, without any discrimination of time, place, or circumstance. Lakshmi herself is said to superintend the dressing of the food, and to taste it before it is served; and, when once placed before the images, it can never be defiled, not even when it has fallen out of the mouth of a dog; much less by the touch of low caste people. The local Mahatmyas are full of stories illustrating its merits. Sufficient to say, that, notwithstanding the strong prejudice of the Hindus against eating rice dressed by other than their own caste men, not only is the rice *Mahaprasad* eaten from the hands of the lowest castes, not excepting Chandals, at Puri; but it is dried and carried to all parts of India for consumption, and at the periodical shraddhas of Vaishnavas, a grain of this holy rice is invariably put on the funeral cake as the most sacred article that can be offered to the manes.*

The quantity of food dressed daily is large; on festive occasions enormous. A considerable profit is made by its sale which goes to the temple funds. The Raja of Khurda sends every day a sweetmeat prepared in his palace at Puri. After consecration, it is sold to pilgrims, and the price credited to the Raja's private account.

Indecent Sculptures.—In the Audience Hall, where pilgrims are admitted to "see god," Dr. R. Mitra says "a few of the human figures are disgustingly obscene."† There are also indecent sculptures on the temple and cars.

The Penal Code contains the following law against obscene books, pictures, and images:

"292. Whosoever sells or distributes, imports or prints for sale or hire, or wilfully exhibits to public view, any obscene book, pamphlet, paper, drawing, painting, representation, or figure, or attempts or offers so to do, shall be punished with imprisonment of either description for a term which may extend to three months, or with fine, or with both."

To prevent the prosecution of Hindu temples, the following exemption had to be made:

"This Section does not extend to any representation sculptured, engraved, painted or otherwise represented on or in any temple or on any car used for the conveyance of idols, or kept or used for any religious purpose."

This is a most lamentable testimony to the character of Hinduism.

Dancing Girls.—There are said to be about 120 dancing girls connected with the temple, who dance for the amusement of the god after his meals. In a memorial to the Lieutenant-Governor of Bengal, they said that they "are greatly needed in pujas and the auspicious performances, and the entertainment of them is closely connected with the management of temples and shrines; from which it is evident that their existence is so related to the Hindu religion that its ceremonies cannot be fully performed without them."

Festivals.—Of these there is a large number; as the Warm Clothing Festival, the Holi, the Birth Festival in which a dancing girl belonging to the temple enacts the part of the mother and a priest that of the father, &c. Only the two most important will be described.

* *Antiquities of Orissa*, Vol. II, p. 129. † *Ibid.*, p. 188.

At the *Snana Yatra*, or 'Bathing Festival,' the images are bathed. After this they are removed to one of the side rooms, where they are kept for a fortnight. This is called the sick room, and the divinities are said to be laid up with fever on account of their annual bath. The outer doors of the temple are closed, and none are admitted. The real object is to clean and repaint the images.

The Car Festival (*Ratha Yatra*) is the great event of the year. It takes place in June or July, and for weeks beforehand pilgrims come trooping into Puri by thousands every day.

THE CAR FESTIVAL AT PURI.

The great car is 45 feet in height, and provided with 16 wheels. The brother and sister of Jagannath have separate cars, a little smaller. When the images are brought out and placed upon their chariots, thousands fall on their knees, and bow their forehead in the dust. The vast multitude shouts with one throat, and surging backwards and forwards, drags the wheeled edifices down the broad street towards the country-house of Jagannath. Music strikes up before and behind, drums beat, cymbals clash, the charioteers shout obscene songs with coarse gestures, which are received with roars of laughter by the crowd. And so the dense mass struggles forward by convulsive jerks, tugging and sweating, shouting and jumping, singing and praying, and swearing. The distance from the temple to the country house is less than a mile; but the wheels sink deep into the sand, and the journey takes several days. The zeal of the pilgrims flags before the garden-house is reached; and the cars, deserted by the devotees, are dragged along by 4,200 professional pullers.

Pilgrims.—There are large numbers of men, called *Pandas*, pilgrim hunters, who go about the country in all directions to entice people to visit Puri, which is called *Swarga-dwara*, the Gate of Heaven. They represent that all sorts of advantages will result from this meritorious act; barren wives will have children, &c. The ground around Puri is said to be all strewn with gold, although, on account of the wickedness of the Kali-yug, it appears to be common dust. Many of these pilgrims are women, who sometimes follow these pilgrim hunters against the consent of their male relatives.

Disease and death make havoc of the pilgrims. During their stay in Puri, they are badly lodged and miserably fed. The priests tell them that they ought not to dress food in the holy city; all must be supplied from the temple. When fresh the food is not unwholesome, although the pilgrims complain of the cooking being often very bad. But unfortunately, only a part of it is eaten fresh, as it is too sacred for the least fragment to be thrown away. Large quantities of it are sold in a state dangerous even to a man in robust health, and deadly to the way-worn pilgrims, half of whom reach Puri with some form or other of bowel complaint. This food is consumed by some one or other, whatever its state of putrefaction, to the very last morsel.

The pilgrims also suffer from bad water. The Puri tanks are all supposed to be extremely holy, and they are also extremely filthy. It is the duty of pilgrims to drink from nearly all of them.

The Car festival happens at the beginning of the rains. On their journey home, pilgrims find every stream flooded, and even those who can pay have often to sit for days in the rain on the bank, before a boat will venture to cross the torrent. Hundreds die upon the roadside. Skeletons lie scattered about the sides of the roads on the principal routes.*

KONARAK, THE BLACK PAGODA.

KONARAK, (*kona*, 'corner' and *arka*, 'the sun'), is situated on the coast, 19 miles north-east of Puri. The following legend is told to account for the erection of the temple: A young man, called Samba, was suspected by the sage Narada to be too familiar with the 16,000 wives of Krishna, so he cursed him and he became a leper. By worshipping the sun daily crying out, "O Surya, O Surya," he was cured. When bathing next day in the river, he found an image, thrown there by Visvakarma, and carved out of a portion of the sun's body. Samba built a temple for the image in which the sun was to be worshipped as the curer of diseases. *Konarak* means the corner of Orissa, dedicated to the sun.

KONARAK, THE BLACK PAGODA.

The temple is said to have been built between 1273 and 1282 A.D. It is now a picturesque ruin, looking down upon the sea. No traces of the outer wall remain, the Marathi officers having carried away the stones as building materials to Puri. Of the temple itself, which in a complete state would have consisted of 4 chambers, only a single one, the Hall of Audience, survives. Its great door-way is blocked up by masses of stone, and festooned by creepers. Sculptures of an indecent character cover the walls. Beautiful women, elephants, warriors on prancing horses, and other figures are represented. A pyramid-shaped roof rises by terraces of carved granite, divided into 3 tiers, to a lotus-crowned pinnacle. The whole is covered with sculptures of elephants, horses, cavalry and foot soldiers in endless processions. The inner edifice seems never to have been completed, as the foundation of internal pillars, on which the heavy dome rested, gave way before the outer halls were finished.

* For a full description of the Temple at Puri, see ACCOUNT OF THE TEMPLE OF JAGANNATH, 'LORD OF THE WORLD', 8vo., 42 pp., 1½ As. Post-free, 2 As. Sold by Mr. A. T. Scott, Tract Depôt, Madras.

GRAND TEMPLE OF BHUVANESWAR.

The enormous pyramidal roof of the still existing outer chamber rests on walls 60 feet high, and rises a further 64 feet above them. It forms a landmark along the coast, for ships on their passage up the Bay of Bengal. The water is shallow, and there have been many wrecks. The villagers explained them by a story of a huge magnet on the top of the tower which drew the unhappy ships on the sands, but they say a Musalman crew at length scaled the temple, and carried off the fatal magnet. It is said that the priests then migrated with their god to Puri.

BHUVANESWAR.

BHUVANESWAR is an inland town, about 20 miles south of Cuttack. It contains about 4,000 inhabitants, many of whom are Brahmans. Once it was the proud capital of a large and flourishing kingdom. The founder was Yayati Kesari, who expelled the Buddhist and established the Kesari or Lion dynasty of Orissa. Yayati began the building of the great temple about 500 A.D. Two succeeding monarchs laboured at it, and the fourth of the house completed it in 657. The Lion dynasty reigned for 6 centuries. One of its last acts was to build the beautiful porch before the temple between 1099 and 1104. The height of the great tower is 160 feet. The name of the presiding deity is Tribhuvanesvara, "the Lord of the three regions,' that is, of the Universe, but the first word of the compound is generally omitted.

Siva is worshipped under the form of a large uncarved block of granite, about 8 feet long, partly buried in the ground, partly apparent above the soil to the height of about 8 inches. The block is believed to be a linga of the Svayambhu class, pervaded of their own nature by the essence of the deity.

The block is bathed with a great profusion of water, as also with milk, and the intoxicating beverage of *bhang*, several times any day, and wiped dry after each washing, offerings of flowers, sandal-wood paste, and new cloth are placed on the block, but other small offerings are put near it, and the divinity is invoked to accept them.

The room in which it is kept is so dark that even at mid-day nothing is visible in it without the help of a lamp. The poorer classes who behold the images from the Dancing Hall can see very little of it. The rich, whose offerings are costly, are allowed to enter the room, to touch the stone, place their offerings thereon, and fan the divinity with a large palm-leaf punka.

"The daily worship consists of no less than 22 ceremonial acts :

(1) At the first appearance of dawn bells are rung to rouse the deity from his slumbers ; (2) a lamp with many wicks is waved in front of the stone ; (3) the god's teeth are cleaned by pouring water and rubbing a stick about a foot long on the stone ; (4) the deity is washed and bathed by emptying several pitchers of water on the stone ; (5) the god is dressed by putting clothes on the stone ; (6) the first breakfast is offered, consisting of grain, sweetmeats, curd, and cocoanuts ; (7) the god has his principal breakfast, when cakes and more substantial viands are served ; (8) a kind of little lunch is offered ; (9) the god has his regular lunch ; (10) the mid-day dinner is served, consisting of curry, rice, pastry, cakes, cream, &c., while a priest waves a many-flamed lamp and burns incense before the stone ; (11) strains of noisy discordant music rouse the deity from his afternoon sleep at 4 P.M., the sanctuary having been closed for the preceding four hours ; (12) sweetmeats are offered ; (13) the afternoon bath is administered ; (14) the god is dressed as in the morning ; (15) another meal is served ; (16) another bath is administered ; (17) the full dress ceremony takes place, when fine costly vestments, yellow flowers and perfumery are placed on the stone ; (18) another offering of food follows ; (19) after an hour's interval the regular supper is served ; (20) five masks and a Damaru, used in dancing, are brought in and oblations made to them ; (21) waving of lights before bedtime ; (22) a bedstead is brought into the sanctuary and the god composed to sleep."

Lastly, the god is sometimes told, "Parvati awaits you."

There is a large tank not far from the temple, called *Vindu Sagara*, because it is said that drops (*Vindu*) from all the sacred pools on earth, in heaven, in the lower regions, as also of nectar, wine, etc., constantly fall into it. The water is of dull green colour, and full of small plants and insects. Kept in a vessel in a quiet place, the water is found to be in motion for hours : a small flower left floating on it, moves about in circles. The ignorant look upon this as a proof of the great sanctity of the water, but it is caused by its impurity. In virtue the tank claims to surpass all other sacred waters. "Whatever merits may be acquired by annual pilgrimages to the source of the Ganges, to Prayaga, or to Ganga Sagar, repeated for 60 years, may be acquired by a single bath in the Vindusagara and the adoration of Mahesvara." "The drinking of the water confers the dignity of Siva, and that dignity lasts as long as the sun."*

Seven thousand shrines once clustered around the sacred lake ; not more than 500 or 600 now remain, and these are nearly all deserted and in ruins.

BUDH GAYA.

Gaya is an ancient city, 57 miles distant by rail from Bankipore, near Patna, on the Ganges. It is divided into two parts, adjoining each other. Old Gaya contains the residence of the priests; Sahibganj is the trading quarter where the civil offices and the dwellings of Europeans are situated. The streets are wide, but the native houses are generally small. The population in 1891 amounted to about 80,000.

Gaya is said to have taken its name from Gaya, an Asura, 567 miles in height, who here practised austerities for many thousand years. The gods, afraid of their supremacy, sought the help of Brahma. By a trick, he persuaded the Asur to lie down, when a heavy stone was placed on him to keep him from moving. As some recompense, however, the gods promised special blessings to persons offering pindas and performing shraddhas at Gaya.

Gaya owes its celebrity chiefly to its connection with Gautama, the founder of Buddhism. What took place there will be described in the section on Buddhist temples. Budh-Gaya or Buddha Gaya, where the temple is situated, is about 6 miles from the town Gaya, on the banks of the Phalgu or Nilaju river.

TEMPLE AT BUDDHA GAYA.

The erection of the original temple is by some attributed to Asoka, the Buddhist king of Magadha, who reigned from 264 to 223 B.C.; but it has been destroyed and rebuilt several times. The stone rail around the temple is probably all that remains of Asoka's erection. Hiouen Thsang, a Chinese Buddhist pilgrim, who visited the temple in the 7th century A.D., after describing the destruction and the subsequent restoration of the bo-tree by the order of the chief queen of Asoka, says that Asoka built a stone wall to surround it, which remained till his day.

In 1876 the king of Burma sent three of his officers to superintend the repairs of the temple. They cleared away a large space around it, built an enclosing wall, and took some steps for preserving the bo-tree. The Bengal Government was afraid lest the Burmese should do serious injury to the

* *Antiquities of Orissa*, Vol. ii., p. 70.

temple by laying bare a part of the foundation. Dr. Rajendralala Mitra, the distinguished Bengali scholar, was therefore sent to Budh Gaya in 1877 to collect information. This led to the publication of his beautifully illustrated work, *Buddha Gaya.* Part of the temple was then in a ruinous condition. It has since been restored and presents the appearance shown in the picture.

Although Buddhism was the dominant religion in India for several centuries, the Brahmans were not entirely overcome, and they gradually regained their influence. Sankar Acharya contributed greatly to this result. Buddha was said to be an incarnation of Vishnu, and, as at Puri, the Great Temple was turned to Hindu account. There is a monastery in the neighbourhood, the mahant of which has, for several generations, had charge of the Temple. He owns a large quantity of land, the revenue from which, with the offerings of the pilgrims, gives him an annual income of about Rs. 80,000.

Shraddhs.—Gaya is now distinguished as the place where Shraddhs can be performed with the greatest efficacy. Performed there, departed relations, wherever they may be, are said to be taken at once to Vishnu's heaven, Vaikuntha.

The Hindu belief about the dead is as follows:—

No sooner has death occurred and cremation of the terrestrial body taken place, than Yama's two messengers, who are waiting near at hand, make themselves visible to the released spirit, which retains its subtle body composed of the subtle elements, and is said to be of the size of a thumb. Their aspect is terrific; for they have glaring eyes, hair standing erect, gnashing teeth, crow-black skin, and claw-like nails, and they hold in their hands the awful rod and noose of Yama. Then, as if their appearance in this form were not sufficiently alarming, they proceed to terrify their victim by fearful visions of the torments in store for him.

The two messengers convey the bound spirit along the road to Yama's abode. There being led before Yama's judgment seat, it is confronted with his Registrar, named Chitragupta. This officer stands by Yama's side with an open book before him. It is his business to note down all the good and evil deeds of every human being born into the world, with the resulting merit and demerit, and to produce a debtor and creditor account properly made up and balanced on the day when that being is brought before Yama. According to the balance on the side of merit or demerit, is judgment pronounced.

Truly the prospect of so terrible an ordeal to a man conscious of his sins might appear absolutely unbearable, were it not for his belief in the doctrine that the ceremonies performed on his behalf by his relations after his death have power, if properly carried out, to turn the scale and perhaps place a considerable balance to his credit.

The disembodied spirit is instantly after its sentence hurried back to the place of cremation. The first object of the Hindu Shraddha is to provide the departed spirit with an intermediate body. Were it not for this, believed to be created by the offerings, the spirit would be an impure and unquiet ghost (Prèta), wandering about on the earth or in the air among demons, and condemned itself to become an evil spirit. The intermediate body converts it from a Prèta into a Pitri, or ancestor. The ball (Pinda) of rice offered on the first day nourishes the spirit in such a way as to furnish it with a head; on the second day, the Pinda gives it a neck and shoulders, and so on. By the tenth day the intermediate body is sufficiently formed to feel the sensation of hunger. On the eleventh and twelfth days it feeds voraciously on the offerings, and so gains strength on the thirteenth day for its terrible journey to Yama.

The wicked man, according to the Garuda Purana, has to travel 86,000 yojanas. Midway is the awful river Vaitarani, 100 yojanas in breadth, of unfathomable depth, filled with blood, infested by huge sharks, crocodiles and sea-monsters; darkened by clouds of hideous vultures. Thousands of condemned spirits stand trembling on its banks. Consumed by a raging thirst, they drink the blood which flows at their feet, then tumbling headlong into the torrent they are overwhelmed by the rushing waves. Finally they are hurried down to the lowest depths of hell to undergo inconceivable tortures.

On the other hand, the Hindu is taught that by performing certain religious rites and giving gifts to the Brahmans, all the terrific penalties of sin may be avoided, and Yama loses his victims. The Brahmans are held for the time to represent the Pitris, and whatever nourishes and benefits the Brahmans, nourishes and benefits the Pitris. It is also thought that the offerers store up merit for themselves as well as help their ancestors. A childless man who has no son to make offerings for him is said to fall into the hell called *Put*. According to Manu, a son was called *putra* by the Self-existent himself because he delivers from *Put*.

The pilgrim who would effectually secure admission for his ancestors into heaven, must scrupulously perform the whole routine of duties, each of which involves presents to the priest. Before leaving his home he must first walk 5 times round his native village, calling upon the souls of his ancestors to accompany him in his journey. Arrived at Gaya, he is forthwith placed in charge of a special Brahman guide, called a Gayawal. There are 45 sacred localities which he should visit in proper order and on particular days. The full round occupies 13 days; but for those who have not sufficient devotion, or sufficient wealth, 38 shrines, two or even only one will serve the desired purpose. The most holy place of all is the Vishnupada temple, supposed to contain a foot-print of Vishnu. At each a *pinda* or ball of rice and water, has to be deposited by the pilgrim, while a hymn is chanted by the attendant Brahman. The number of pindas varies with the number of ancestors, for whom the Shraddhas are celebrated, and the size of the balls and the materials of which they are composed differ according to the caste and the country of those who perform the rite. The pindas are left to be eaten by birds and other animals or deposited in the river.

The amount spent in fees to the rapacious Gayawals is sometimes enormous. The late Maharaja of Kashmir is said to have expended at least Rs. 15,000 on the Gayawal priests before their desires were satisfied. Towards the end of the last century a Peshwa is said to have expended a lakh of rupees.

Evils of Shraddhs.—The expense is a serious consideration. Sir Monier Williams justly remarks :

" In truth, the expenditure of time, money, and energy needed to satisfy public opinion before a man is held to have discharged the debt due to a deceased father, and before he is relieved from the long course of fasting and mourning he is expected to undergo, constitutes an evil which has gradually grown till it has become a veritable curse to the country, and one of the principal bars to any advance in its social condition. Nor is there any warrant for the system in the more ancient books held sacred in India as authoritative guides."

The moral evils are even worse than the poverty. Numbers of idle vagabonds, some of them notoriously vicious, are maintained who should work for their living. The impression is given that a man's welfare in another world depends mainly, not upon his own conduct, but on the offerings made after his death. He may lead any sort of life, however immoral and wicked, provided he leave enough to feed the Brahmans, and especially to have his Shraddha performed at Gaya. Thus encouragement is given to sin. On the other hand, a childless man is said to fall into *Put*. The great Judge of all the earth will do that which is right. A man will be rewarded or punished for his own deeds, not for those of others over which he has no control.

The whole system is clearly an invention of the Brahmans to deceive ignorant credulous Hindus and get their money. At a time when mourning the loss of relatives, they work upon their feelings, and extort from them all they can.

It is our duty to cherish the memory of our forefathers, but their happiness in a future state depends upon their own conduct—not upon our offerings. The best way of showing respect for them is by living noble lives.

BENARES TEMPLES.

To the Hindu, Kasi is the most sacred spot on earth. The Hindus, indeed, affirm that it is not built on earth, but on a point of Siva's trident. At one time it is said to have been of gold; but in the Kali Yug it has been turned into stones and mud. Though the Ganges is supposed to be sacred during its entire course, as it flows past Kasi, its cleansing power is believed to be vastly increased. The rites performed there have double efficacy : the very soil is fraught with blessing. All who die within *Panch Kosi*, or within a circle of 10 miles around the city, are sure to go to heaven, whatever may have been their character.

Pilgrims, when they first get a glimpse of the holy city, raise shouts of *Jai, jai Kasinath*, "Victory to the lord of Kasi!" Some, not deeming it sufficiently respectful to enter it on foot, prostrate themselves on the ground, measuring it with their bodies. Individuals have been known to come great distances in this way.

BENARES. RAJA OF AHMETY'S TEMPLE. BURNING GHAT WITH SATI STONES.

Benares is situated on the northern bank of the Ganges, about 120 miles below its junction with the Jumna. It is 476 miles from Calcutta by rail ; from Bombay, viâ Allahabad, it is 938 miles ; from Madras the distance is 1,550 miles.

The city stretches for about four miles along the northern bank. The river, more than a third of a mile in width, sweeps round like a half moon. Along the northern bank a precipitous cliff rises to the height of 100 feet ; the opposite bank is low, and is flooded by the river during the rains.

For several centuries Benares was the headquarters of Buddhism. The city then lay around Sarnath, to the north of the Barna. After a time Hinduism began to recover its hold. The Brahmans adopted several Buddhist doctrines, and pretended that Vishnu appeared as Buddha to encourage wicked men to despise the Vedas, reject caste, and deny the existence of the gods to their own destruction. Sankar Acharya, who lived in the 8th or 9th century, by his disputations with the Buddhists and his writings, did much to promote the worship of Siva in Benares. In the eleventh or twelfth century, the Buddhists seem to have been finally expelled.

It may be said of Benares, like Athens of old, that it is "wholly given to idolatry," and that it contains more idols than human beings. In some places there are great accumulations of images.

The temples also are almost numberless, though some of them are very diminutive. Raja Man Singh, of Jeypore, wishing to present a lakh of temples to the city, made the stipulation that they were all to be commenced and finished in one day. The plan hit upon was to cut out in blocks of stone a great many tiny carvings, each one representing a temple. The separate blocks, therefore, on the work being completed, exhibited from top to bottom and on all sides a mass of miniature temples. These blocks are still to be seen in various parts of Benares.

THE BISESHWAR OR GOLDEN TEMPLE.

But there are numerous temples more deserving of the name. The Muhammadan Sultan Ala-ud-din, about 1300 A.D., is said to have destroyed about a thousand temples; but they so multiplied again that they rose to about 1,500. Jehangir, the fourth Mogul emperor (1605-27), in his memoirs describes Benares as a "city of temples." These again, in their turn, were levelled by Aurungzeb (1658-1707). A third time they raised their heads, and their number is now estimated at 1,550, besides very numerous smaller shrines.

The largest temples in Benares were demolished by the Muhammadans. Those existing are much inferior in size to some of the temples in South India. But though small, the Benares temples are generally solidly built of hewn stone, and some of them are richly carved. Siva's temples are surmounted by his trident. Many have a pole at their side, with a flag attached to it.

The temples are generally situated either along the bank of the river or a little inland; some of them are clustered together.

Supposed Proof of the Sanctity of Benares.—On one occasion Brahma and Siva quarrelled about their respective positions. As Brahma declared that he was supreme, Siva cut off his fifth head, and thus was guilty of the most heinous crime of injuring a Brahman,

Brahma being the progenitor of the Brahmans. After giving vent to his anger, Siva found himself in a most miserable plight: the dissevered head of his rival adhering to his hand. In order to get free from this dreadful sign of his revengeful spirit, Siva wandered from shrine to shrine, and practised the most severe penances; but all was in vain until he reached the sacred city of Benares. There he lost his burden; and following his example, his worshippers, weighed down with the burden of sin, go from shrine to shrine; but in Benares, of all other places, imagine that they find peace of conscience and the assurance of salvation. The money-lender whose life has been spent in grinding the poor, the unjust judge whose right hand is full of bribes, the liar, the thief, the adulterer, the murderer, hope by coming to Benares to procure forgiveness, and die deluded by their false hope.

Three of the principal temples will be noticed.

Bisheshwar Temple.—The name Bisheshwar is applied to Siva as "lord of all." The whole city is supposed to be dedicated to Siva. He is supposed to be king over all the other deities as well as the inhabitants residing within the limits of the Panch Kosi road. Every matter of importance is supposed to be brought to the notice of Siva by his Kotwal, Bhaironath. The idols placed along the road are supposed to act as chaukidars or watchmen.

The temple was erected by Ahalya Bai, Maharani of Indore. It stands in the midst of a quadrangle, covered in with a roof. Over it are a tower, a dome, and a spire. The tower and dome glitter in the sun like masses of burnished gold, and on this account it is called the Golden Temple. It is merely gilded with gold leaf spread over plates of copper, overlying the stones beneath. The expense was met by Ranjit Sing in his last illness, in the vain hope of prolonging his life.

The tower is 51 feet in height. Outside the enclosure is a large collection of idols, raised upon a platform, and called "The Court of Mahadev." They are chiefly male and female emblems. Other idols are built into the wall flanking this court. They were probably taken from the ruins of the old temple of Bisheshwar, destroyed by Aurangzeb, which stood to the north-west of the present building. Extensive remains of the old temple are still visible. They form a large portion of the western wall of the mosque which was built on its site.

Under the dome is a belfry, in which 9 bells are suspended. These are so low that they can be tolled by those who frequent the temple. One of them, of elegant workmanship, was presented by the Raja of Nepal.

The image of Bisheshwar is the Linga, similar to that which is found in all Saiva temples. All day long crowds of people of all classes pass in front of this symbol with their offerings of sugar, rice, ghee, grain, flowers, money, &c., which are taken by the ministering priests as their own. Over the narrow gateway leading to the shrine is an image of Ganesa, on which the pilgrims sprinkle as they pass a few drops of water they have brought from the river. A bell is hung in front of the image, which is kept sounding all day long, by which the attention of the deity is supposed to be called to a worshipper as he goes to pay his respects.

Near the Temple is the Ġyan Kup, or "Well of Knowledge." The legend is that once the rains were withheld for 12 years from Benares. The people being in great distress, a Rishi pierced the earth with Siva's trident, where there issued a copious stream of water. Siva hearing of this, promised to reside in the well for ever after. It is said that when the old temple of Bisheshwar was destroyed, the priest took the chief idol and threw it down the well for safety. The well is surrounded by a roofed colonnade of about 40 beautiful pillars, erected in 1828 by the widow of Daulat Rao Sindhia of Gwalior.

The well is now covered except a small portion. The water is filthy and putrid from the rotted flowers thrown into the well by those who resort to the shrine. Every pilgrim drinks a little handed to him in a sort of ladle by one of the attendant priests. On payment, the priest also repeats a mantra.

To the east of the colonnade there is a stone bull, about 7 feet high, the gift of the Raja of Nepal. Near it is a temple of Siva, built by a Hyderabad Rani.

Bhaironath.—This temple is upwards of a mile north of the Golden Temple, and not far from the Town Hall. The god is supposed to be the *Kotwal*, or police magistrate, of Benares and its suburbs as far as the Panch Kosi road. Within this limit, under his master Bisheshwar, he exercises authority over gods and men. It is his special duty to expel evil spirits. He himself is guarded by a huge dog, although it is said to enable him to indulge occasionally in riding exercise. The sweetmeat sellers in the neighbourhood make sugar images of the dog which are offered to this idol.

DURGA, OR MONKEY TEMPLE, BENARES.

The god is armed with an enormous stone club, called *Dandpan*, from *danda*, a stick. It is about 4 feet in height, with a small silver face at the thin end. This stick has been commanded to beat every disturber of the peace. It is specially worshipped on Tuesday and Sunday. Three bells hang in front of the stick, and on one side sits a priest, with a rod made of peacock's feathers. In the name of Dandpan, he gently taps the worshippers with this rod, which punishment is considered sufficient to absolve them from all their sins.

Durga.—The temple of this goddess lies at the southern end of the city. The Skanda Purana gives the following account why the wife of Siva assumed this name :

Kartikeya being asked by Agastya, the sage, why his mother was called Durgā, said : "A giant, named Durga, the son of Ruru, having performed penance in favour of Brahma, obtained his blessing, and grew so mighty that he conquered the three worlds, and dethroned Indra and the other gods. He compelled the wives of the Rishis to sing his praise, and sent the gods from heaven to dwell in the forests, and by a mere nod summoned them to reverence him. He abolished religious ceremonies ; Brahmans through fear of him gave up the reading of the Vedas ; rivers changed their course ; fire lost its energy ; and the terrified stars retired from sight. He assumed the shape of the clouds, and gave rain whenever he pleased ; the earth through fear yielded an abundant harvest, and the trees flowered and gave fruit out of the proper season.

"The gods in their distress appealed to Siva. Indra, their king, said 'He has dethroned me !' Surya said, 'He has taken my kingdom !' Siva, pitying them, desired Parvati to go and destroy this giant. She, accepting the commission willingly, calmed the fears of the gods, and first sent Kalaratri (Dark Night), a female whose beauty bewitched the inhabitants of the three worlds, to order the giant to restore all things to their ancient order. The giant, full of fury, sent some soldiers to lay hold of Kalaratri ; but by the breath of her mouth she reduced them to ashes. Durga then sent 30,000 other giants, who were such monsters in size that they covered the surface of the earth. At the sight of these giants, Kalaratri fled through the air to Parvati, followed by the giants. Durga, with 100,000,000 chariots, 120,000,000,000 elephants, 10,000,000 swift footed horses, and innumerable soldiers, went to fight Parvati on the mountain Vindhya. As soon as the giant drew near, Parvati assumed 1,000 arms, and called to her assistance different beings, and produced a number of weapons from her body (a long list of these is given in the Purana). The troops of the giant poured their arrows on Parvati sitting on the mountain Vindhya, thick as the drops of rain in a storm ; they even tore up the trees, mountains, &c., and hurled them at the goddess, who threw a weapon which carried away many of the arms of the giants. Durga hurled a flaming dart at the goddess, which she turned aside ; another being sent, she stopped it by a hundred arrows. He then sent an arrow at Parvati's breast ; this too she repelled, and also two other weapons, a club and a pike. At last Parvati seized Durga and set her left foot on his breast, but he, disengaging himself, renewed the fight.

"The beings when Parvati caused to issue from her body then destroyed all the soldiers of the giants. In return Durga sent a dreadful shower of hail, the effect of which Parvati counteracted by an instrument called Sosuna. The giant now assumed the shape of an elephant as large as a mountain, and approached the goddess, but she tied his legs, and with her nails, which were like swords, tore him to pieces. He then arose in the form of a buffalo, and with his horns cast stones, trees, and mountains, tearing up the trees by the breath of his nostrils. Parvati next pierced him with her trident, when he reeled to and fro, and renouncing the form of a buffalo assumed his original body as a giant, with a thousand arms, and weapons in each. Approaching Parvati, she seized him by his thousand arms, she carried him into the air, whence she threw him down with fearful force. Seeing that this fall had not injured him, she pierced him in the breast with an arrow, when blood issued from his mouth in streams, and he died. The gods were delighted and soon regained their former splendour. Parvati, in honour of her victory, assumed the name Durgā."

The above account is from a Saiva Purana. The Vaishnava Puranas give other accounts, and glorify Vishnu. All are equally incredible, and can be accepted as true only by people little children in intellect.

Some account will now be given of the temple of Durgā Kund at Benares. The temple, which is built of stone richly carved, was erected last century by the Mahratta Rani Bhavani. This she did in addition to repairing the Panch Kosi road. The porch was the gift of a Native officer. The main entrance to the temple passes through the Naubutkhana, which contains the large drum, that is sounded three times a day in honour of the goddess. The upper part of the building being open on all sides, permits the sound to travel forth. On either side of the entrance rise two small shrines, and in the space between them is placed the altar and the wooden post, to which the animals about to be sacrificed are tied. At the porch lie waiting, as it were, the sculptured figures of two lions in crouching attitude, intended for the use of the goddess whenever she wishes to take a ride. Grouped around are smaller buildings, devoted to Ganesa and Mahadeva. The central one contains the cell with the image of Durgā, and the high pointed tower with its graceful ornaments forms the roof. The whole quadrangle is surrounded by high walls, and on the sides of the enclosure there are raised terraces, that were built for the convenience of pilgrims.

As Durgā is delighted with the sight of flowing blood, goats and kids are offered to her. After the head has been cut off and some blood presented, the body is taken away by the worshipper, and may be eaten. This is allowed by the Sastras. In return for the blood, Durgā is supposed to deliver from sickness and other affliction.

On account of the monkeys found there, Europeans called it the *Monkey Temple*.

The monkeys scamper over the tops of the houses, and wherever their fancy leads them, sitting on walls and many other places from which they may watch their opportunities for stealing the property of their human fellow-creatures. They are revered as representatives of the god Hanuman, and are fed with various kinds of grain, distributed by the worshippers as a work of great merit. When any person scatters grain, crying out, *ao*, *ao*, 'come, come,' the monkeys soon collect in numbers.

On account of the mischief done by the monkeys, some years ago a Magistrate of Benares removed a large number of them to the jungles.

Adjoining the temple there is a fine *Kund*, or tank, much used for bathing.

Muttra and Brindaban.

Muttra (*Mathura*) is situated on the western bank of the Jumna, about 30 miles above Agra. The central portion of the Muttra District forms one of the most sacred spots in Hindu mythology. The circuit of 84 *Kos* around Gokula and Brindaban bears the name of the Braj Mandal. Here Krishna and Balarama are said to have fed their cattle.

In the Mahabharata generally Krishna is little more than a hero. In the Bhagavad Gita, a production of later date now held to be part of the great epic, he claims to be the Supreme Being. He says: "All this universe has been erected by me; all things exist in me." The popular idea of him is chiefly derived from the Bhagavat Purana, a Hindu version of which, known as *Prem Sagar* (the Ocean of Love), is very popular. The following is an abridged account of his history:

It is said that Kansa, king of Muttra, was a great enemy to cows and Brahmans. Upon this the gods sought the assistance of Vishnu, who, listening to their request, plucked off two of his hairs, which he said would assume incarnations and destroy Kansa. The white hair became Balarama, and the black one, Krishna.

Balarama and Krishna were born the seventh and eighth sons of Vasudeva and Devaki. A voice from heaven had told Kansa, that he would die by the eighth son of Vasudeva, and he sought therefore to destroy all his male children. Krishna, born at midnight, had a very dark skin. The gods lulled the guards to sleep, and Vasudeva, stealing out undiscovered, went across the Jumna with the child. There he found the cart and oxen of a cowherd, named Nanda, whose wife Yasoda, had just been delivered of a female child. Vasudeva took away the female infant, and left his own son. Nanda brought Krishna to the village of Gokula.

Many wonderful stories are told of the childhood of Krishna. A female demon, Putana, disguised herself as a very beautiful woman, and having put poison on her breast, tried to suckle him. Krishna, when placed on her bosom, sucked her life with the milk till she fell down dead.

Balarama and Krishna were brought up together in the village of Gokula or Braja. Krishna and his companions, children of the cowherds, amused themselves by going into houses when the people were out, stealing butter, eating some of it, and throwing the rest about. As he did this day

KRISHNA WITH BUTTER.

after day, the wives of the cowherds hid themselves, and caught Krishna when he came to steal. Afterwards they went and complained to Yasoda. They told about his thefts, and that when any one pointed to the curds on his mouth, Krishna said that the same person had placed them there. When Yasoda questioned Krishna, he said that the wives of the cowherds had spoken falsely, and accused them of treating him unkindly.

One day when Yasoda was churning milk, Krishna, who had been asleep, awoke and cried for food. As Yasoda did not come at once, he, in a passion, took the butter out of the churning dish, threw it about, besmeared his body with it, and kicked with his feet. When Yasoda offered him some food, Krishna said, "I will not take any now; why did you not give it me at first?" As soon as Yasoda went out to look after the milk that was boiling over, Krishna broke the vessels containing the curds, and, having filled a small pot with butter, ran off to the children of the cowherds. Afterwards, when Yasoda was crying, Krishna declared that he did not know who spilt the buttermilk.

Kaliya, the snake-king, lived in a pool in the Jumna. Krishna, it is said, leaped into the pool, took out the snake, trampled upon his hood, till blood gushed out of his mouth, and afterwards allowed him to go to the ocean.

KRISHNA AND THE SNAKE.

The story is well known of Krishna stealing the clothes of the wives of the cowherds when they were bathing, and obliging them to come to him naked. He used also to dance and sport with them.

In ancient times, in this country, Indra was considered the chief of the gods. Krishna taught the cowherds that, as they were supported by their cattle, they ought to make them their chief divinity. Indra, angry because he was neglected, poured down a flood of water upon the people. Krishna, to deliver them, plucked up the mountain Govardhana, and held it up, like an umbrella, for seven days on the point of one of his fingers.

Afterwards Krishna killed Kansa, and placed his father, Ugrasena, on the throne. A powerful foreign king invaded the country on the Jumna, whereupon Krishna went to Gujarat, and built the city Dwaraka on the coast. He married Satyabhama, and carried off by force Rukmini. He had eight queens, and sixteen thousand wives. The number of his sons is said to have been 180,000.

When on a visit to Indra's heaven, Satyabhama incited Krishna to steal the famous Parijata tree, produced by the churning of the ocean, which was then growing in Indra's garden.

The Mahabharata relates that Krishna, Balarama, their wives and children, and all the Yadavas, with abundance of wine and meat, went to Prabhasa to hold a great feast. Becoming intoxicated, they began to fight. Fathers killed sons, and sons fathers. All the sons of Krishna perished. Only he and Balarama were left alive, and they resolved to become ascetics. Balarama soon afterwards died, and when Krishna was reclining in the jungle, a hunter, mistaking him for game, pierced his foot with an arrow, causing his death.

Some of the principal events in the history of Krishna, have been briefly described. To the present time, Krishna is worshipped by millions of people, who hope by him to obtain the happiness of heaven. Let us examine for a little his history.

When Krishna was a child, he is said to have been frequently guilty of theft. When charged with it, he told lies. He disobeyed Yasoda, and like a spoiled child, broke dishes and refused to eat. Krishna is worshipped, even as a boy, under the name of Balkrishna. Will any worshipper of Krishna dare to set the example of the god before his own children? Would not a child guilty of disobedience, lying, and theft, be deserving of severe punishment? If he said that these things were done in sport, would this be admitted as an excuse? Krishna's worshippers allege that he was a god, and could do as he pleased. This makes his conduct only the worse, The greater the agent, the greater the offence.

Were a king to forbid his subjects from committing a certain crime, and yet be guilty of it himself, would he not be worthy of blame? He would, in truth, be more culpable than any of his subjects. If a great teacher were to give his disciples excellent precepts, and yet violate them himself, would his conduct not be condemned? In like manner, were God himself to break His Holy laws, how could He punish sinners? There is a proverb, *yathá devah, tathá bhaktah,* As is the god, such is the worshipper. The example of Krishna can only corrupt his followers.

Hear what the one true God says: "Thou thoughtest that I was altogether such an one as thyself; but I will reprove thee." God is spotless in holiness; He commands children to obey their parents; He forbids lying, theft, drunkenness, and adultery. Can we suppose that, if incarnate, He would have been guilty of such acts Himself? The very thought is a great sin. All such stories as are related of Krishna are the inventions of wicked men, who framed gods after their own evil hearts. There are no such gods, and it is very sinful to worship them.

A few of the principal places in the Braj Mandal will be noticed.

MUTTRA is a very ancient city. About 400 A.D., Fa Hian, the Chinese pilgrim, mentions it as a centre of the Buddhist faith. Another pilgrim, 250 years later, says that it then contained 20 Buddhist monasteries and 5 Brahmanical temples. It was sacked by Mahmud of Ghazni, with terrible atrocity, in 1017-18. About 1500 Sultan Sikandar Lodi utterly destroyed all the shrines, temples, and images; and in 1636 Shah Jahan appointed a governor expressly to "stamp out idolatry" in Muttra. In 1669-70 Aurungzeb visited the city and destroyed many temples and shrines. In 1756, under Ahmad Shah Abdali, 25,000 Afghan horsemen swooped down upon Muttra during a festival, when it was thronged with peaceful Hindu pilgrims. They burned the houses together with the inmates, slaughtering others with sword and lance, hauling off into captivity maidens and youth, women and children. In the temples they slaughtered cows, and smeared the images and pavement with blood.

Muttra is still visited by numerous pilgrims. Swarms of monkeys infest the streets, and the river is full of turtles, both fed as a work of merit.

GOKUL is a village on the east bank of the Jumna, about 6 miles below Muttra, celebrated as the scene of Krishna's childhood. It is also noted as the place where Vallabhi Swami first preached his doctrines in the 16th century. Near it is MAHABAN, containing the so-called palace of Nandi. Krishna's supposed cradle, a coarse structure covered with red calico and tinsel, still stands in the pillared hall, while a blue-black image of the child looks out from a canopy against the wall. The churn in which Krishna's foster-mother made butter is shown, and consists of a long bamboo sticking out of a carved stone. The place is visited annually by thousands of Vishnu-worshippers, with yellow-stained clothes.

BRINDABAN is 6 miles above Muttra, on the same side of the river. It is regarded as one of the holiest cities of the Hindus. It contains a large number of temples and shrines. The temple of Gobind Deva, erected about 1590 A.D., by Raja Man Singh of Amber, is among the finest Hindu buildings in India. The body is in the form of a cross. The centre is crowned by a beautifully proportioned dome. There are 3 other temples of the same period, known as Gobinath, Jugal Kishor, and Madan Mohan. They are in the same style, but inferior in proportions, and in a much more ruinous condition. The gorgeous modern temple which dominates the town was built by two brothers, Muttra Seths, Govind Das and Radha Krishna. The former became a devotee in 1874. Every day more than 100 persons are fed at this temple. There are 3 gopuras, or gate towers, in the outer wall, 80 feet high, covered with sculptures of very inferior workmanship. The outer court not only encloses the temple and inner court, but a fine garden and tank, with steps leading down to the water on all four sides. In front of the god is a huge pillar of copper, gilt, rising 60 feet, and sunk 24 more in the ground. The copper cost Rs. 10,000. The temple was begun in 1845, took 6 years to complete, and cost about 50 lakhs.

Here Krishna is said to have stolen the clothes of the women of Bruj, and to have danced with the cowherdesses.

TEMPLE AT KHATMANDU, NEPAL.

NEPAL is a large independent state on the Himalayas, between Tibet and British territory. It is about 500 miles in length; the breadth varies from 70 to 150 miles. The area is estimated at 54,000 square miles—rather more than that of Assam—and the population at 2 millions.

The country is very mountainous. It contains Mount Everest, 29,002 feet above the sea, the loftiest known peak in the world. The whole northern frontier rises to the height of perpetual snow. Lower down, there are narrow valleys, from 3,000 to 6,000 feet above the plains of Bengal.

TEMPLE IN KHATMANDU.

The inhabitants belong chiefly to various tribes of Tartar or Chinese origin, bearing no resemblance to the Hindus either in features, religion, or manners. The Gurkhas are the ruling race. They are said to have emigrated from Tirhut in the 14th century A.D. Their language resembles Hindi; but about $\frac{1}{5}$ of the words have been adopted from Tibetan, &c. They worship chiefly the goddess Kali. They form only a small proportion of the population. They are little men, but very brave soldiers. The Indian army contains some Gurkha regiments.

Khatmandu, the capital, is situated in a valley, about 4,500 feet above the sea. The population is about 50,000. The name is said to be derived from an ancient building which stands in the heart of the city near the royal palace. *Kath* means 'wood,' the material of which it is chiefly composed, and *mandi*, a 'building,' or 'temple.' The houses, which are usually from 2 to 4 storeys high, are made of bricks, and tiled; many of them possess large projecting wooden windows, often richly carved. The streets are narrow and dirty.

The Maharaja's palace is a large building in the centre of the city. Part of it is very old, built in pagoda fashion, and covered with elaborate and grotesque carvings. In the square in front of the palace are numerous handsome temples. Many of these are like pagodas, of several storeys in height, and profusely ornamented with carvings, paintings and gilding. The roofs of many of them are entirely of brass or copper gilt, and along the eaves of the different storeys are hung numerous little bells, which tinkle in the breeze. At some of the doorways are placed a couple of large stone lions, with well-curled manes.

Close to the palace on the north is the temple of Taliju, one of the largest of the pagoda type. It is said to have been built by Raja Mahendra Male, about 1549 A.D. It is devoted entirely to the use of the royal family. Not far from the palace, and close to one of the temples is an enormous bell, suspended from stone pillars; and in another building are two huge drums, about 8 feet in diameter. The bell is sounded by pulling the tongue, but the peal is by no means what might be expected from its size. Here, too, are several huge and hideous figures of Hindu gods and goddesses which on festival days are dressed up and ornamented in the usual way.

GANGOTRI TEMPLE.

Machchhindranatha is considered the guardian deity of Nepal. The following is the legend: Nepal had suffered from a drought 12 years, which threatened to be the ruin of the country. Narendra Das, a Nepal Raja, therefore went to Assam about 437 A.D., to invite an eminent Buddhist saint. To do him honour, Brahma swept the road, reciting the Vedas as he did so; Vishnu blew the sankha; Mahadeva sprinkled water on the road; Indra held an umbrella; Yama lighted the incense; Kuvera scattered riches; Agni displayed light; Vayu held the flag; and Ishan scared away demons. Copious rains fell on the arrival of the saint, and the country was saved from famine.

In memory of this visit, Narendra Das built a temple, and called it after Machchhindranatha, as the saviour of the country. He also instituted an annual festival, which is still celebrated as the greatest of all the national festivals. On the last day the blanket of Machchhindranatha is shaken before the people to show that he carries nothing away from them, and that, though in poverty, he is contented.*

Gangotri Temple.

The Himalayas (the abode of snow) form an immense wall 1,500 miles in length, 200 in breadth, and about 4 miles in height, curving round the north of India. From the plains at some distance, the mountains look like a long row of white clouds, topping the lower wooded ranges which rise out of a belt of haze.

At the foot of the hills, there is a narrow marshy tract, called the Tarai, affording pasture to innumerable herds of cattle and buffaloes, but fever-stricken, and in some parts infested with wild beasts. Beyond is a range of hills about 3,000 feet in height, covered with forests of the valuable *sal* tree. Next there are in some parts fertile well-watered valleys, called *Dhuns*, extending to the foot of the true mountains. Another range of mountains then rises rapidly to the height of about 8,000 feet. On the ridges are placed stations frequented by Europeans during the hot season. As we ascend, trees gradually diminish in size, till at the height of about 3 miles even shrubs disappear, and perpetual snow covers black naked rocks.

The Himalayas are of great benefit to India. Vapour from the ocean falls upon them in the form of snow. The heat of the sun melts the snow which flows down in countless streams, swelling the rivers in the plains, so that they are in flood in the hottest season of the year when the moisture they supply is most needed. They also act like a screen against the cold wind from the north.

Ignorant people in various countries have imagined lofty inaccessible mountains to be the abodes of their deities. The Greeks placed their gods on Olympus, the highest mountain in their country. In the Puranas, the Himalayas are placed to the south of the fabulous mountain Meru, while Kailasa, to the west, is described as a mountain of pure silver, the residence of Siva.

Unenlightened nations have a tendency to worship what is useful to them instead of adoring their great Creator. In Egypt the river Nile is of still greater importance than the Ganges is in India: without it the whole country would be a desert. The ancient Egyptians therefore made a god of the river. The Ganges is similarly worshipped.

The Puranas represent the Ganges as flowing from the toe of Vishnu, and to have been brought down from heaven by the prayers of the saint Bhagiratha, to purify the ashes of the 60,000 sons of the king Sagara, who had been burnt by the angry glance of the sage Kapila. Hence the river is called Bhagirathi. Ganga was angry at being brought down from heaven, and Siva, to save the earth from the shock of her fall, caught the river on his brow, and checked its course with his matted locks. The descent of the Ganges disturbed the sage Jahnu as he was performing a sacrifice, and in his anger he drank up the waters, but he relented and allowed the water to flow from his ear: hence the Ganges has the name Jahnavi. Ganga, as a goddess, is the eldest daughter of Himavat, the Himalayas; her sister is Uma. She became the wife of king Santanu, and bore him a son, Bhishma, also called Gangeya. In a peculiar way she became the mother of Kartikeya.

The mouth of the Ganges at Ganga Sagar, and its source at Gangotri, in the state of Garhwal, are considered peculiarly sacred. The temple is high up in the Himalayas, 8 miles from the source of the river. The river is commonly believed to flow out of a cow's mouth, but actually from an ice cave at the foot of a bed of snow. The temple contains images of Ganga, Bhagirathi, &c. Pilgrims regard it as the limit of their journey. There are no houses

* Wright's *History of Nepal, &c.*

in the neighbourhood. Pilgrims therefore soon leave, taking with them a flask of Ganges water which is sealed by the officiating priest, and carried to the plains as a valuable treasure.

The water of the Ganges is no more sacred than that of any other river. We do not require to make long toilsome journeys to worship God. "The Most High dwelleth not in temples made with hands." "He is not far from any one of us; for in Him we live and move, and have our being." Wherever we are, He is always ready to listen to our prayers.

KEDARNATH.

KEDARNATH, like Gangotri, is in Garhwal. The name is applied to a snowy peak of the Himalayas, 22,853 feet in height, and also to a famous temple on its side, more than 11,000 feet above sea-level. It is said to mark the spot where an incarnation of Siva, after fighting his numerous battles, attempted to dive into the earth to escape his pursuers, the Pandavas. He left his lower limb above the surface in the shape of a holy rock,—the remaining portions of his body being distributed elsewhere. Close to the temple rises a precipice known as Bhairab Jhamp, where devotees formerly committed suicide by flinging themselves from the summit, till the practice was suppressed by the British Government. With Kedarnath are included 4 other temples in the neighbourhood, the whole forming the Panch Kedar, a famous round of pilgrimage, containing the scattered portions of Siva's body. One of the great lingams is said to be at Kedarnath.

BADRINATH.

BADRINATH, not far from Kedarnath, is held to be still more sacred. The peak rises to the height of 23,210 feet above the sea. From the glaciers on its sides, the Alaknanda river, one of the principal tributaries of the Ganges, takes its rise. The temple of Vishnu, also called Badrinath, stands on one of the shoulders of the mountain, at an elevation of 10,400 feet. The temple is said to have been erected by Sankara Swami, who brought up the figure of the deity from the bottom of the river, after diving 10 times. It consists of a conical building, surmounted by a small copper-covered dome, ending in a golden ball and spire. Below the shrine a sacred tank stands on the hill-side, supplied with water from a hot spring. Pilgrims of both sexes bathe in the sacred pool. Immense numbers of pilgrims annually pay a visit to Badrinath.

HARDWAR.

HARDWAR is situated on the Ganges, where it issues from the

HARDWAR.

mountains. The Vaishnavas called it *Hari-dwara*, 'Vishnu's Gate'; the Saivas, *Hara-dwara*, 'Siva's Gate.' It was undoubtedly a sacred spot long before either Vaishnavism or Saivism assumed its present form.

The great attraction is the bathing ghat, with the adjoining temple of Gaya-dwara. The foot-mark of Vishnu, cut on a stone, let into the upper wall of the *ghat*, forms an object of special reverence. Each pilgrim struggles to be the first to plunge into the stream after the propitious moment has arrived, and strict police regulations are required to prevent the crowd trampling one another and drowning each other. In 1819, 430 persons, including some sepoys on guard, lost their lives by crushing in this manner; after which accident Government constructed the present enlarged *ghat* of 60 steps, 100 feet in breadth. The great assemblage of pilgrims takes place on the first day of the month Baisakh, the commencement of the Hindu Solar year, and the supposed anniversary of the day upon which the Ganges first appeared on earth. Every 12th year a feast of peculiar sanctity occurs, known as a *Kumbh-mela*, and is attended by an enormous concourse of people.

Last century, before Hardwar came under British rule, there were sometimes great fights between the pilgrims. In 1760, on the last day of bathing, the rival mobs of the Gosain and Bairagi sects had a long continued battle, in which some 1,800 are said to have perished. In 1795 the Sikh pilgrims slew 500 of the Gosains. Such fights have ceased, but cholera sometimes breaks out among the pilgrims, and they scatter the disease along the principal lines of travel.

THE OILMAN'S TEMPLE, GWALIOR.

The GWALIOR TERRITORIES, under Sindhia, form the largest of the Central India States. They include detached districts between the Chambal and the Narbada, larger than Mysore, with a population of about 3 millions. Some parts in the north are hot, rocky and sandy; the southern districts in the tableland of Malva, are cool and fertile. The founder of the Sindhia family was Ranoji Sindhia, the slipper-bearer of Balaji Peshwa, at the beginning of last century. His father was the headman of a Deccan village. Once in the household of the Peshwa, Ranoji's rise was rapid, and he soon found himself at the head of the body-guard. After leading many Marathi raids, he was at the time of his death the acknowledged possessor of lands which still form part of the Gwalior State.

GWALIOR, the capital, is 65 miles south of Agra. It is noted for its hill fort, on an isolated rock, a mile and a half in length, 300 yards in breadth, and 340 feet high. The old town of Gwalior is of considerable size, but irregularly built and very dirty. It contains the remains of two famous temples. One of them, being Jain, will be described under another head.

THE OILMAN'S TEMPLE is supposed to have been so called because erected by a wealthy oilmonger. It is 60 feet square, with a portico in the east projecting about 11 feet, and terminating in a ridge of about 30 feet in extent. It was originally dedicated to Vishnu, but afterwards converted to the worship of Siva. It was probably built on the 10th or 11th century.

NASIK.

NASIK is the Benares of Western India, and plays the same part to the Godavari river as Benares does to the Ganges. It is situated on both banks of the Godavari, about 30 miles from its source. To induce pilgrims to come to it, the Brahmans have invented the most remarkable stories regarding the river. Its sacredness is said to have been revealed to Rama by the Rishi Gautama. The popular belief is that it proceeds from the same source as the Ganges by an underground passage. Every part of its course is holy, and to bathe in its waters will wash away the blackest sin.

The river at Nasik is about 80 yards broad, flowing through a succession of shallow masonry basins, with flights of stone steps for the use of bathers and pilgrims. The banks are lined with temples, shrines, and dharmsalas, and many others rise in the middle of the shallow river.

Nasik is claimed to be the place where Rama passed his long period of banishment. The temple, called Panchavati (the five banyans) is celebrated throughout all Western India. It is situated on the eastern bank of the river, about half a mile outside the town. It stands under the shade of 5 large banyan trees, and none but Hindus may enter it. Panchavati is claimed to be Nasik, because Lakshman cut off Surpanakha's nose (*násika*) at Panchavati!

TELI-KA MANDIR. 'THE OILMAN'S TEMPLE,' GWALIOR.

The Sundar Narayan temple is a beautiful temple, built about the beginning of last century. The oldest temple in the town is that dedicated to Siva, under the name of Kapaleshwar, the lord of skulls. It is ascended by 50 steps, and is 600 years old. The handsomest

TEMPLES ON THE GODAVARI AT NASIK.

temple is that dedicated to Bala Rama, standing in an oblong enclosure with 96 arches, 260 feet long, and 120 broad. The shrine in the centre is 93 feet by 65, and 60 feet high. It is about a hundred years old, and is said to have cost 7 lakhs.

The various stone basins through which the river passes are called *Kunds*. That on the Panchavati side is Rama's Kund, where it is said he was wont to bathe. The ashes of the dead are thrown into the river from its steps.

As rival shopkeepers brag about the superior excellence of their goods, so the Brahmans on the NARBADA or *Narmada* (bliss-giver), claim that it is superior in sanctity to the Godavari and even to the Ganges. It is said to have sprung from the perspiration of the god Rudra. "One day's ablution," they say, "in the Ganges frees from all sin, but the mere sight of the Narbada purifies from guilt. Furthermore, either bank of the Narbada may be used for burning the dead, whereas only the northern bank of the Ganges is effectual for that purpose."

ROCK-CUT TEMPLES.

The CAVE TEMPLES of India are one of its greatest marvels. No other country in the world possesses such a magnificent group of rock-cut monuments. The period during which the people of India were given to making these excavations is supposed to have begun about 250 B.C., and to have ended about 800 A.D. The earliest are Buddhist; next are the Brahmanical caves; and lastly those of the Jains.

There are in Western India upwards of 50 groups of rock-cut excavations, of which upwards of 900 have been described. The great majority are within the limits of the Bombay Presidency or in its immediate borders. Besides these, there are a few insignificant groups in Orissa, Sind, the Panjab, Baluchistan, and Afghanistan.

The explanation of their number in the Bombay Presidency is probably found in the trap rocks, which overlie the country and form the hill sides everywhere in the West, being exceptionally well suited for the purpose. They lie everywhere horizontally; they have alternating strata of harder and softer rocks which admit of caves being inserted between them with singular facility. The labour of excavating a rock-cut temple in so suitable a material is probably less than would be required to erect a similar building in quarried stone.

PORCH OF KAILAS TEMPLE, ELLORA.

The Buddhist excavations date from the middle of the 3rd century B. C., to near the 7th century of our era, thus ranging through 9 or 10 centuries. Besides being the oldest, they are the most numerous. About 720 have already been described.

The Brahmanical excavations range from about the 4th to the 8th century of our era, or perhaps later. They amount in number to about 160, but several of them are of considerable size, whereas, many of the early Buddhist caves are insignificant.

The Jain Cave Temples may belong from the 5th or 6th century down to the 12th. They number only about 35.

The principal Brahmanical cave temples will now be described.

The **Ellora Temples** are situated in the north-west of the Nizam's dominions, about 13 miles from Aurangabad. Rozah, where the Emperor Aurangzeb died, is not far from Ellora. The caves are excavated in the sloping sides of the hill, running nearly north and south for a mile and a quarter, each end throwing out a ridge towards the west. The Buddhist caves, of which there are 12, are in the south; the Brahmanical caves, of which there are 17, besides smaller ones, are in the centre; while 5 Jain caves are in the north. Waterfalls descend in front of the caves, and the base of the mountain is fringed with brushwood and trees.

The principal building is called KAILAS after Siva's heaven. It is not like an ordinary temple built with stone added to stone, but a large solid rock has been hewn into a temple. It contains a series of caves as large as churches, with huge images 8 or 10 feet high, ranged round the walls, elephants, lions, alligators, antelopes, swans and oxen larger than life. They are varied by intricate wall sculpture of every description, the whole carved out of the solid rock, without a single stone being introduced.

On the sloping side of the hill, a pit has been dug out, forming a court, 100 feet deep at its inmost side, 150 feet wide, 270 feet long. On the floor of this pit stands the temple. At the entrance of the court there is a gateway. A bridge leads from this to a large square porch shown in the picture, with pillars on either side, and connected by a second bridge with the central buildings. Crossing the bridge, you enter a square room in which is the Nandi Bull. This room has 2 doors and 2 windows. Opposite the windows are two beautiful square towers, 38 feet high, graduated from the base to the capitals, which were originally crowned with lions. Two elephants, the size of life, have also been carved out of masses of stone left standing in the court.

From the Bull the visitor crosses over another bridge and enters the grand apartment, through a doorway guarded by 2 gigantic sentinels in stone. At the end is the Lingam; the whole of the hall is elaborately sculptured.

In a verandah there are 43 groups of Hindu divinities, with sculptures illustrating their history. The first of the Brahmanical caves is called Ravana Ka Khai. It is full of sculptures representing scenes in the history of Durga, Lakshmi, Siva, Parvati, &c. The Das Avatar is the oldest Brahmanic cave, and bears evidence of having been begun by Buddhists and finished by Brahmins. The great chamber is 103 feet by 45 feet, sustained by 46 pillars.

The Kailas temple is supposed to have been erected about the 8th century by Raja Edu of Ellichpur, as a thank-offering for a cure effected by the waters of a spring near the place.

CAVES OF ELEPHANTA.

ELEPHANTA is an island in Bombay harbour, about 6 miles from the city. It is nearly 5 miles in circumference, and consists of two long hills, separated by a narrow valley. It was named *Elephanta* by the Portuguese, from a large stone elephant which stood near the old landing place on the south side of the island. This elephant was about 13 feet in length and 7 feet high; but its head and neck dropped off in 1814, and subsequently the body sank down into a shapeless mass of stones, which were removed in 1864 to the Victoria Gardens in Bombay. Except on the north-east and east, the hill sides are covered with brushwood; below is a belt of rice land. At one period, from the 3rd to perhaps the 10th century, the island is supposed to have been the site of a city, and a place of religious resort.

The island is noted for its caves. Of these wonderful excavations, four are complete or nearly so; a fifth is a large cave now much filled up, with only rough masses of stone left to support the roof. The most important is the Great Cave, situated in the western or larger of the 2 hills of the island, at an elevation of about 250 feet above high water level. The entrance is reached by a winding path, about ¾ of a mile from a landing-place. The cave faces the north, and is entirely hewn out of hard rock. From the front entrance to the back,

ENTRANCE TO THE GREAT CAVE, ELEPHANTA.

it measures about 130 feet, and its length from the east to the west entrance is the same. It does not however occupy the entire square of this area. Three massive columns cut out of the

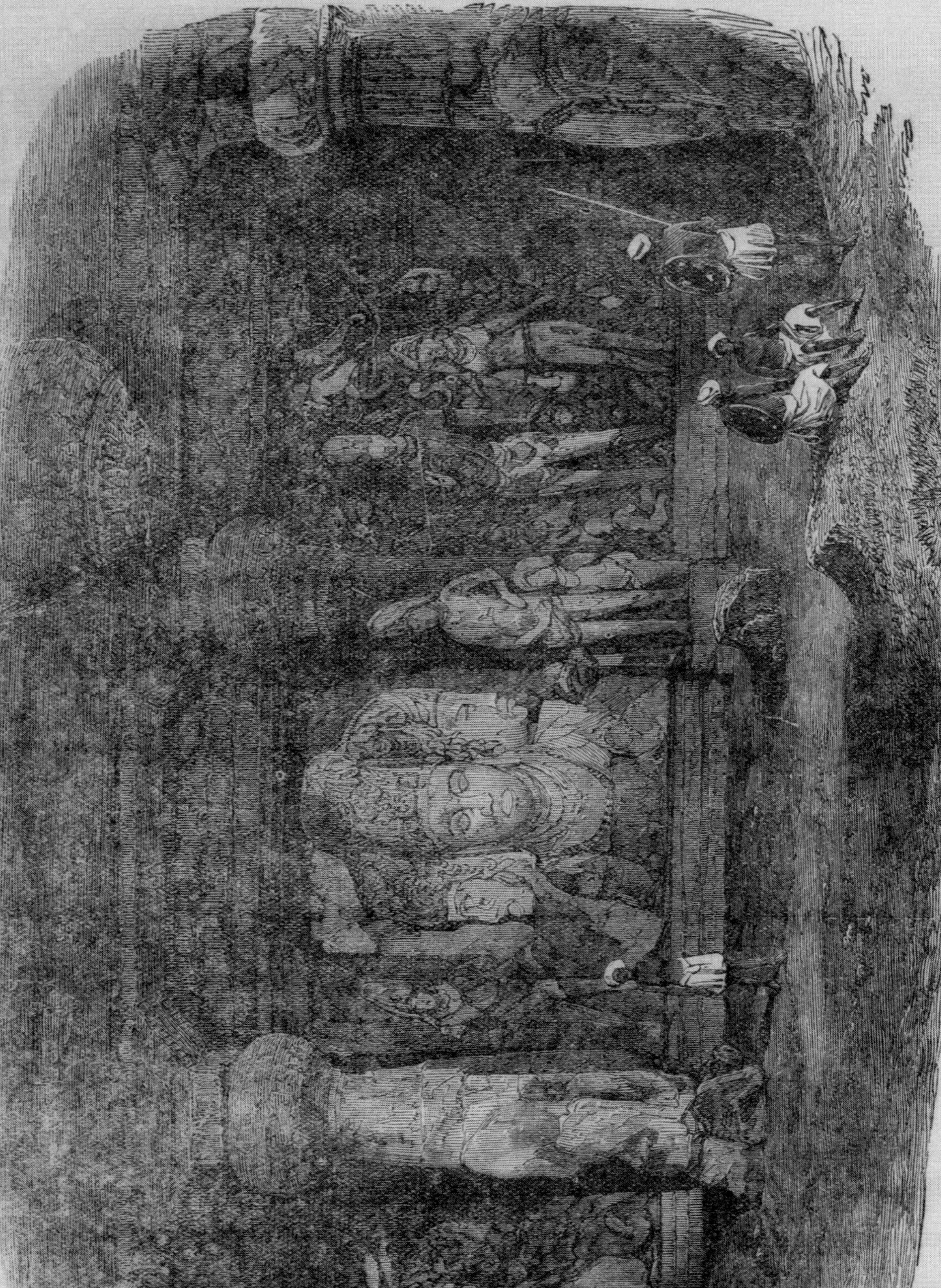

THE TRIMURTI IN THE GREAT CAVE, ELEPHANTA.

ENTRANCE TO THE TIGER CAVE, ELEPHANTA.

rock, divide the entrance, and support a huge overhanging cliff, covered with verdure and flowering creepers.

The body of the caves may be considered a square of about 91 feet each way, supported by 6 rows of columns. There were originally 26 columns, with 16 half columns, but 8 of the separate pillars have been destroyed, and others are much injured. As neither the floor nor the roof is perfectly horizontal, the columns vary in height from 15 to 17 feet. The most striking of the sculptures is the famous colossal *Trimurti*, at the back of the cave, facing the entrance. This is a representation of Brahma, Vishnu and Siva, as the creative, destructive, and preservative principles. Brahma is the embodiment of *rajas*, passion, desire, by which the world was called into being; *Sattva*, goodness, by which the world is preserved; and *tamas*, darkness or anger, by which the world is annihilated. The *Trimurti* is nearly 18 feet in height. It is guarded by two gigantic *dwarapalas*, or door-keepers, of rock, about 13 feet high: both figures are much defaced. The linga chapel, on the right-hand side of the temple on entering, contains several *dwarapalas* and other figures; and two compartments on either side of the *Trimurti* are also ornamented with numerous sculptured groups.

The compartment to the east of the *Trimurti* contains gigantic figures, grouped about a gigantic *Ardhanari* or Siva represented as a half male, half female divinity. The figure is nearly 17 feet in height. In the compartments to the west are two figures of Siva and Parvati. In another compartment is represented the marriage of Siva and Parvati, in which she stands at his right hand, a position which the wife rarely occupies except on her marriage day.

On the right-hand side of the temple is the compartment containing the linga, guarded by gigantic door-keepers. The bull which stood facing it in the court has disappeared. In a compartment in the west end of the cave, there is a figure of Siva as *Kapalabhrit*, 11½ feet high. There is a skull in the headdress, and a rosary of skulls hangs in front. This is Siva as Bhairava.

The Tiger Temple is about 50 feet in length and 18½ feet in height. It is divided into 5 spaces, by 4 columns and 2 pilasters. On each side of the steps leading up to the temple are bases, on which stand tigers. Inside them is a *garbha* or *linga* shrine, with various figures.

There are three other temples in a ruinous state.

There are no inscriptions on the temples. They are supposed to have been executed about the 9th century of the Christian era. The Great Temple is still used on Sivite festivals, especially by banyas. A mela is held here at the Sivaratri.

Bombay Presidency.

Western India is notorious for the infamous Vallabhi sect of Vaishnavas. The chief priests, called Maharajas, are regarded as incarnations of Krishna. Men and women prostrate themselves at their feet, offering their incense, fruits, and flowers, and waving lights before them. It is believed that the best way of propitiating Krishna in heaven is by ministering to the sensual appetites of the Maharajas. Body, soul, and property (*tan, man, dhan*), are to be wholly made over to them. Women are taught to believe that the highest bliss will be secured to themselves and their families by intercourse with the Maharajas. Rich Bombay merchants, as shown at a trial in 1862, gave their wives and daughters to be prostituted as an act of religious merit to men who had ruined their health by debauchery.

Mr. M. Malabari gives the following as some of the taxes which Maharajas exact from their wealthy followers :-

"For homage by sight, Rs. 5; for homage by touch, Rs. 20; for the honour of washing the Maharaja's foot, Rs. 25; for the honour of swinging him, Rs. 40; for the glory of rubbing sweet unguents on his body, Rs. 42; for the joy of sitting with him, Rs. 60; for the bliss of occupying the same room, Rs. 50 to 500; for the performance of the circular dance, Rs. 180 to 200; for the delight of eating the *pan supari* thrown out by the Maharajah, Rs. 17; for drinking the water in which the Maharaja has bathed, or in which his foul linen has been washed, Rs. 19."*

Pandharpur and Jejuri.

Exclusive of Nasik, two of the most noted temples in the Bombay Presidency are at these places.

* *Gujarat and the Gujaratis*, p. 122.

Pandharpur is situated in the Sholapur district, south-east of Bombay. It contains a celebrated temple, now dedicated to Vithoba. The legend is that a pious Brahman had a most undutiful son, named Pundalik, who vexed his parents in all possible ways. He reformed, however, and became as noted for his devotion to them. One day Krishna came to Pandharpur in search of his wife Rukmini, who, justly offended at his unfaithfulness, had forsaken her husband, and fled to this place. Krishna hearing of Pundalik's love of his parents, paid him a visit, and found him washing his father's feet, which employment he continued notwithstanding the presence of the god. Delighted with his piety, Krishna told Pundalik to ask any boon he pleased. He, still intent on serving his father, merely requested the god to remain where he was, and there he is to this day, standing upon the brick with which Pundalik had been rubbing his father's feet, and which, on recognising the god, he had thrown down for him to sit upon. He is represented with his hands still resting on his loins, just as when wearied with his long search for Rukmini, he appeared to Pundalik.

This is reason to believe that Vithoba, now worshipped as an incarnation of Vishnu, was one of the Jain saints. The image is *digambar*, sky-clad or naked, though a regard for modesty has made the Hindus dress him in yellow garments, the colour adopted by Buddhist priests.

The temple, 350 feet long and 170 in breadth, is near the centre of the part of the town which is considered holy, and is called *Pandarikshetra*, the holy field of Pandhari. Vithoba is sometimes called *Pandharinath*, the lord of Pandharpur.

Jejuri is a village about 24 miles from Poona, the chief seat of the worship of Khandoba, one of the most popular gods in Western India. He is said to have been a raja, who was regarded as an incarnation of Siva. He is sometimes represented with his wife on horseback, attended by a dog. The wicked custom prevails of dedicating children to his service. A couple, having no family, vow that if Khandoba will help them, their first child will be his. If a boy, he grows up a "dog of Khandoba," and wanders about as a vagrant. If a girl, after undergoing ceremonial "purification," she is branded with a heated stamp, and is married to the god with the pomp of a Hindu marriage. Such women, called Murlis, are simply prostitutes.

Somnath, or **Pattan Somnath,** is an ancient town in the Junagarh State, in the south of Kathiawar, near the port of Verawal. On the edge of the sea, nearly half way between the two towns, stands a large and conspicuous temple, dedicated to Siva. It occupies a lofty and projecting rock, whose base is washed by the ocean. For a considerable distance around the temple, the whole space is now occupied by portions of columns, sculptured stones, and other fragments of the original building.

When the temple was in all its glory in 1026 A.D., it was attacked by Mahmud of Ghazni. The archers of Mahmud soon cleared the walls of their defenders, and the Hindus dispirited, leaving the ramparts, prostrated themselves before the symbol of their god, imploring his aid. The assailants applied their scaling ladders and mounted the walls amidst shouts of Allah Akbar (God is great); but the Hindus rallied, and the soldiers of Mahmud had to fall back. On the third day, however, the Hindus having been defeated in a great battle, the garrison made their escape by a gate towards the sea, although not without considerable loss.

Mahmud, his sons, and a few of his nobles entered the temple. He beheld a superb edifice of hewn stone, its lofty roof supported by pillars curiously carved. In the innermost shrine, to which no external light penetrated and which was illuminated only by a lamp suspended from the centre by a golden chain, appeared the linga, which rose 9 feet in height above the floor of the temple. Brahmans offered an immense sum if Mahmud would spare the linga, one of the 12 great ones; but he said that he would be known by posterity, not as "the idol seller," but as the "idol destroyer." Fragments were broken to be sent to Ghazni. Mecca, and Medina.

Dwaraka (*The City of Gates*) is situated at the western extremity of the Kathiawar peninsula. The Vishnu Purana says that the Yadavas, the tribe to which Krishna belonged, having been very much weakened, he built the city of Dwaraka, defended by high ramparts and beautified with gardens and reservoirs of water, crowded with houses and buildings, and splendid as Amaravati, the capital of India. Thither Janarddana conducted the inhabitants of Mathura.

"On the same day that Krishna died, it is said that the ocean arose and submerged the whole of Dwaraka except alone the dwelling of the deity of the race of Yadavas. The sea has not yet been able to wash that temple away, and there Kesava constantly abides even to the present day. Whoever visits that holy shrine, the place where Krishna pursued his sports, is liberated from all sin."

The Hindus believe that the temple was raised in one night by supernatural agency. It consists of a shrine, a spacious hall of audience, the roof of which is supported by 60 granite and sandstone pillars, and a conical spire 170 feet in height. The body of the temple has 5 storeys, its height being 100 feet.

SOUTH INDIAN TEMPLES.

As far back as traditions reach, we find the DRAVIDA DESA, or southern part of India, divided into 3 kingdoms, the PANDIYAS, the CHOLAS, and the CHERAS. Of the three the most southern was the Pandiyan Kingdom, the earliest civilized. It had acquired sufficient importance about the time of the Christian era to have attracted the attention of the Greek and Roman geographers. Its capital was Madura. The Chola Kingdom had its headquarters successively at Kumbakonum and Tanjore. Talkad, in Mysore, now buried by the sands of the Kaveri, was the capital of the Chera Kingdom.

The Dravidians were great temple-builders. The Saivas predominate in South India, but the Vaishnavas are also numerous. Fergusson has the following remarks on the South Indian Temples :—

"There does not seem to be any essential difference either in plan or form between the Saiva and Vaishnava temples in the south of India. It is only by observing the images are emblems worshipped or by reading the stories represented in the numerous sculptures with which a temple is adorned that we find out the god to whom it is dedicated. Whatever he may be the temple consists almost invariably of the four following parts arranged in various manners, but differing in themselves only according to the age in which they were erected :

1. The principal part, the actual temple itself, is called the *Vimána*. It is always square in plan, and surmounted by a pyramidal roof of one or more storeys ; it contains the cell in which the image of the god or his emblem is placed.

2. The porches or *Mantapas,* which always cover and precede the door leading to the cell.

3. Gate pyramids, *Gopuras,* which are the principal features in the quadrangular enclosures, which always surround the *Vimánas.*

4. Pillared halls, or *Choultries,* used for various purposes, and which are the invariable accompaniments of their temples.

GOPURA OF A TEMPLE AT PERUR, NEAR COIMBATORE.

Besides these, a temple always contains tanks or wells for water—to be used either for sacred purposes or the convenience of the priests—dwellings for all the various grades of the priesthood attached to it, and numerous other buildings designed for state or convenience.*

There is one most disgraceful feature connected with some of the South Indian temples. Dubois referring to them, says:—

"Next to the sacrificers, the most important persons about the temples are the dancing girls, who call themselves *deva-dasi*, *servants* or *slaves of the gods*. Their profession requires of them to be open to the embraces of persons of all castes.

"They are bred to this profligate life from their infancy. They are taken from any caste, and are frequently of respectable birth. It is nothing uncommon to hear of pregnant women, in the belief that it will tend to their happy delivery, making a vow, with the consent of their husbands, to devote the child then in the womb, if it should turn out a girl, to the service to the Pagoda. And, in doing so, they imagine they are performing a meritorious duty. The infamous life to which the daughter is destined brings no disgrace on the family."

According to the Puranas, there is a similar class in Indra's heaven, the Apsaras, called *Surángañás*, "wives of the gods," and *Sumad-átmajás*, "daughters of pleasure," who are common to all.

Two thousand years ago the Greeks had a religion somewhat like that of the Hindus. Their gods fought with each other, and committed adultery. The temple of Venus at Corinth had more than a thousand *hierodouloi*, "servants of the goddess," who were the ruin of many a stranger who visited the city. For several centuries this went on unchecked. Well might it be said by Bishop Lightfoot:

"Imagine, if you can, this licensed shamelessness, this consecrated profligacy, carried on under the sanction of religion and in the full blaze of publicity, while statesmen and patriots, philosophers and men of letters, looked on unconcerned, not uttering one word and not raising one finger to put it down."

The same remark applies to India. Now, happily, through the Christian influence which is insensibly purifying Indian public opinion, a movement has sprung up against nautch women, and their employment in temple services has been condemned.

Like the temple of Jagannath at Puri and others in Orissa, some of the South India temples have most indecent sculptures.

An account will now be given of a few of the principal temples.

TIRUPATI.

TIRUPATI is about 90 miles north-west of Madras. The town at the foot of the hill is known as *Lower* Tirupati, and the temple on the hills as *Upper* Tirupati. The mountain has 7 principal peaks. Near one of them, named Seshachellam, stands the temple, and the whole range *Tirumalai*, is often called after this particular peak. The hills are said to have originally formed part of Mount Meru. This change in locality is said to have arisen from a dispute between Adi-Shesha, the thousand-headed serpent, and Vayu, the god of the winds, as to which was the more powerful. To show his strength, Adi-Shesha lifted one of the peaks of Mount Meru upon one of his heads, but Vayu raised so terrible a tempest with his breath that the peak was blown away, and falling to the earth formed the Tirupati hills!

The chief temple is 6 miles distant from Lower Tirupati, but the outer entrances begin about a mile from the town. There are 31 *tirtams* or pools of water, all more or less sacred. The Swamipushkarani is a large tank about 100 yards by 50, surrounded with cut stone steps, and situated close to the temple. Every pilgrim bathes in its green filthy water. Once a year the waters of all the sacred rivers and tanks of India are asserted to unite together, and on that day Swamipushkarani is said to be much swollen. Bathing in it at this time is held to be a sure mode of purification from all sin.

The principal road to the temple is that from Lower Tirupati. All classes may go as far as a large gopuram, but beyond this none but caste men can proceed. Until lately no European was allowed to go inside the temple. In 1870 in an enquiry into a murder case, an

* *Indian and Eastern Architecture*, pp. 324, 325.

English Magistrate entered the temple. At the gopuram begins a long flight of stone steps leading up to Tirumalai. The temple is surrounded by three stone walls, and rising in the centre of the space is seen a rather insignificant dome. The size of the enclosure is 137 yards by 87 yards. The shrine is a small chamber, lighted only by lamps, containing the idol, a standing representation of Vishnu in stone, 7 feet in height. It has 4 arms. One on the right hand holds the mace, and one on the left the chank; the other right hand points to the earth to draw attention to the miraculous origin of the holy mountain, while a lotus is grasped in the remaining left.

The building of the temple is attributed to Tondima Chakravarti, who lived near Kalahastri, about 16 miles distant. Siva is supposed to have been originally worshipped, but Ramanujacharya, it is said, procured a chank and chakram of gold which he placed before the image, and closed the temple doors. When they were next day opened, they were found grasped in the idol's hands, which was regarded as a proof that he was Vishnu! Pilgrims generally come with the cry of "Go-o-o-o-vinda," but some from the north call the idol Balaji, after a Brahman supposed to be an incarnation of Vishnu.

Sickness and the desire of male offspring are the chief causes which induce persons to make a vow to the Tirupati idol. A very common offering of the women is the hair of their heads, and there is a spot not far from the large porch where barbers shave these votaries, and the hair forms an enormous pile. More than half the women who return from visiting the shrine appear with clean shaven heads.

The income of the temple was formerly 2 lakhs a year, and it is still considerable. A hundred of the principal inhabitants of Tirupati presented a petition to the Viceroy calling attention to the lamentable waste of the temple funds. Money is spent in maintaining a host of idle, able-bodied vagabonds. *The Hindu* says, "The vast majority of these endowments are corrupt to the core. They are a festering mass of crime and vice, and gigantic swindling."*

CONJEVERAM.

CONJEVERAM, or KANCHIPURAM, is 46 miles south-west of Madras. It was an important city of the Chola Kingdom, and in the 14th century the capital of Tondamandalam. After the fall of the Vijayanagar family in 1644, it was subject to the Muhammadan kings of Golconda, and at a later date became part of the Arcot dominions. In 1751, Clive, returning from Arcot, took the town from the French.

Conjeveram is one of the seven holy cities of India, a pilgrimage to which is supposed to confer happiness in heaven. When visited by a Chinese pilgrim in the 7th century A.D., it was a great Buddhist centre; but the following century, it was Jain, and Jain nuns are still to be seen in the district. About the 12th century the place fell under Hindu predominance, and the Vijayanagar Rajas, who had treated the Jains liberally, endowed the sacred places of their own religion with great magnificence. Two of the temples, among the largest in South India, were built by Krishna Raya about 1509.

The two towns of *Great* and *Little* Conjeveram possess groups of temples, choultries and all other features of a place frequented by pilgrims.

The huge Saiva temple at Great Conjeveram has some noble gopuras, large mandapas, the usual 1,000 pillared hall, and some fine tanks, with flights of stone steps. The largest gopura has 10 storeys, its height being 188 feet; it is nearly as possible square at the base, each side being about 74 feet. The summit affords a fine bird's eye view of the entire temple and surrounding country, but is rather a fatiguing ascent, the steps being very high and the passages so dark that torches are necessary.

The hall, said to count 1,000 pillars, numbers only 540. Most of the columns are beautifully carved. In the centre of the hall are a number of grotesque wooden figures, used for processional purposes.

The Vishnu temple of Little Conjeveram is about 2 miles distant from the Great Temple. Here is a very remarkable hall of pillars, 96 in all, carved at the basis into horsemen and fabulous animals. In front of the tank are 2 columns for flagstaffs, and a beautiful pavilion with a painted roof resting on 4 slender pillars. The treasury of this temple is rich in ancient jewels.

* May 31st 1894. The account of the temple is chiefly abridged from the *North Arcot Manual*.

Chidambaram.

Chidambaram, (or more correctly *Chittambalam*, 'the atmosphere of wisdom'), is about 150 miles south of Madras, and 7 miles from the coast. It is chiefly noted for its temples. The great temple is sacred to Siva and Parvati. Tradition says that the earliest portions of this vast structure were built by Hiranya Varna Chakrasti, the golden colour king, who was cured of leprosy by bathing in a tank at this place. This splendid group of buildings measures 600 yards by 500 yards, covering 39 acres. Two walls, each 30 feet high, surround it; and at each of the 4 corners stands a gopura 122 feet high, faced with granite blocks 40 feet long and 5 feet thick, covered with copper. The temple of Ganesa is said to contain the largest image of the god in India. There is a curious chain, 27 feet long, cut out of a single stone.

The temple belongs to about 250 families of a peculiar sect of Brahmans, 20 of whom are always on duty at a time for a period of 20 days. These Dikshatar Brahmans marry only among themselves. They collect alms all over South India when not on duty in the temples.

Kumbakonam.

Kumbakonam, (the water-jar mouth) is situated in the Tanjore District, about 190 miles south-west of Madras. It was formerly one of the capitals of the Chola kingdom, and noted for its learning. The Gopura of the largest temple is in 12 storeys, and is fully 160 feet high. The temple of Siva is approached by a curious arched passage, 330 feet long, lined with shops on either side. The Mahamaham tank has its banks studded with temples, flights of steps, and a very large temple of red brick. There are a large number of huge idol cars which at the annual festival are dragged by thousands of people. Every twelve years the waters of the Ganges are said to flow into this tank; when vast numbers bathe in its muddy water.

Tanjore.

Tanjore is situated in what is called the Garden of South India. It is in the delta of the Kaveri, and surrounded by a network of irrigation canals.

Tanjore was the last capital of the Chola dynasty, and was afterwards ruled by a Naik governor from Vijianagar. Between 1656 and 1675, it fell into the hands of the Mahrattas.

The state was acquired by the British in 1779, and in 1855 the capital lapsed on the death of Raja Sivaji.

The great temple consists of 2 courtyards, the outer 250 feet square, and the inner about 500 feet by 250 feet, in which the temple itself stands. The buildings date from the beginning of the 14th century, and onwards.

The central tower of the temple is the finest in India of its kind. Its base is a square of 96 feet, and the height 208 feet. The huge circular dome at the top is formed of one mass of granite. Tradition says that an inclined plane of 5 miles in length was built up which this enormous stone was rolled to the top of the tower by forced labour.

The gateway tower is one of the oldest portions of the temple. It is dedicated to Siva. It was built about 1330 A.D., by one of the Kings of Conjeveram. Halfway between the entrance gate and the great temple is the famous Nandi. The pillared shrine is shown to the right in the picture. The bull is 16 feet long, and 12 feet high, sculptured out of a solid block of rock, said to have been brought a distance of 400 miles. It is daily anointed with oil, which makes it shine like the finest bronze.

A peculiarity of the temple is that all the sculptures on the *gopuras* belong to Vishnu, while everything in the courtyard is dedicated to Siva.

On the north side of the great tower is a temple dedicated to Subrahmanya, a younger son of Siva. Against one of its outer walls is placed a water spout. The water which flows from it has been poured over the idol inside, and is drunk by worshippers as a meritorious and purifying act.

SRIRANGAM.

SRIRANGAM, often called Seringham by English writers, is a town on a island of the Kaveri, 2 miles north of Trichinopoly. The southern arm of the river retains its name; the northern is called the Coleroon or Kolladam. The island is reached by a long bridge of 32 arches, each of 60 feet span. The town is noted for the temple of Vishnu, the largest in India. The double walls enclose an area 960 yards long by 825 yards wide. The great northern *gopura* is 130 feet wide at its base, by 100 feet in depth. The passage through it is 21½ feet wide, and 43 feet high. The gate posts are granite monoliths, and the roofing slabs are 24 feet long. Its present height is under 200 feet; if it had been finished, it would have risen to a height of 300 feet.

The central enclosure is small and insignificant, and except that the dome is gilt has nothing to distinguish it from an ordinary village shrine. The next enclosure, however, is more magnificent. It includes the hall of columns, which measures some 450 feet by 130 feet. The pillars are each of a single block of granite and more or less elaborately carved.

The next 4 enclosures have nothing very remarkable in them, being generally inhabited by Brahmans and persons connected with the temple. The outer enclosure is practically a market, filled with shops where pilgrims are lodged and fed. At a distance, the 14 or 15 great towers have an imposing effect. There are several beautiful tanks and gardens. The whole of the buildings belong to the 17th and 18th centuries, many of them being unfinished. The entire fabric is supposed to be a terrestrial counterpart of Vaikuntha, Vishnu's heaven.

Srirangam is celebrated as the residence of Ramanuja, founder of the Vasishtadwaita philosophy. He is said to have lived for 120 years, and to have died in 1137. One of the temple courts contains a shrine of Ramanuja.

MADURA.

MADURA is situated on the south bank of the river Vaigai, 344 miles by rail south-west of Madras. It is one of the most ancient and celebrated cities in India. The Pandyas were established at Madura at least as early as the 5th century B.C., and their empire lasted

MADURA GOPURA.

till the end of the 11th century A.D. The last of the line, named Sundara Pandya, or Guna Pandya, is said to have exterminated the Jains, and conquered the neighbouring Chola Kingdom; but he was in his turn overthrown by an invader from the north.

Subsequently the district became a province of the great Hindu empire of Vijayanagar. In the 16th century, Visvanath, the founder of the Nayak dynasty, was sent from Vijayanagar as ruler of Madura. His greatest successor was Tirumala (1623-57), who adorned Madura with many public buildings. After his death his kingdom gradually fell to pieces. In 1740 Madura was taken by Chunda Sahib. In 1801 it was ceded by the Nawab of the Carnatic to the English

Madura was anciently famous for its college. Siva, it is said, gave the professors a diamond bench which extended itself to receive all worthy of a place, and pushed off all mere pretenders. Tiruvalluvar, a Pariah priest, author of the best ethical poem in any Indian language, appeared as a candidate for a seat; but the Brahman professors would not give him a place. When the poem was laid on the bench, it so expanded as to throw all the occupants off! The professors were so sensible of their disgrace that they drowned themselves in a neighbouring tank; and so the college came to an end.

THE TANK, MADURA TEMPLE.

The great Madura Temple, dedicated to Sundareswara and his wife Minakshi, is 282 yards long and 248 yards broad, with 9 gopuras, one of which is 152 feet high. The thousand pillared hall was built by Arya Nayak about 1550. The tank is surrounded by arcades, and is very beautiful.

The vimana, or central shrine, was built by Viswanath about 1560. The whole interior of the temple is one mass of carving, the sculptures of Madura being the finest in India.

THE TEPPAKULAM, MADURA.

Tirumala's Choultry, is a pillared hill, 111 yards long by 35 wide, with 4 ranges of columns, 120 in all, each of which differs from the other, and all most elaborately sculptured. The front is adorned with groups of warriors on rearing horses, slaying men or tigers, &c. It was built by Tirumala as a guest house for Siva, who consented to pay the king an annual visit of 10 days on condition that a hall worthy of his dignity was built for his reception.

There are 10 groups of sculptured figures, some large, others small, representing Tirumala and his 9 predecessors, with their wives.

The Teppakulam, a large tank about 1½ mile east of the city, is also assigned to Tirumala. It is a square each side, measuring 1,200 yards, or not far from a mile. The banks are faced with hewn granite, and surmounted with a handsome parapet, also of granite. In the centre rises a square island, with a lofty domed temple in the middle, and a small shrine at each corner. Once a year the banks of the tank are illuminated with a lakh of lamps; while the idols from the pagoda are drawn round in a *teppam,* or raft, from which the tank takes its name.

Rameswaram.

Rameswaram is a low sandy island in the Gulf of Mannar, now separated from the mainland, by a narrow strait, called the Paumben. It is about 11 miles long by 6 wide, and was probably at one time connected with the mainland. The eastern half is merely a narrow strip of sand. The temple, claimed to be founded by Rama himself, is one of the most celebrated in India. It is associated with Rama's journey to Ceylon in search of Sita. Thousands of pilgrims come from all parts of India through Ramnad to the crossing. It is to

TEMPLE AT SRIVILLIPUTUR, IN THE TINNEVELLY DISTRICT.

their control of the passage from the mainland that the chiefs of Ramnad owe their hereditary title of Setupati, "Lord of the Bridge or Causeway."

The temple stands on a rising ground in the northern part of the island, in a quadrangular enclosure, about 600 feet long and 157 feet broad, and is entered by a gateway, 100 feet high. The temple is enclosed by a wall 22 feet high, with 4 *gopuras*, one on each side, which have this peculiarity, that they are built wholly of stone, from the base to the summit. The western one alone, however is finished. Those on the north and south are hardly higher than the wall in which they stand. Their progress was probably stopped by Muhammadan and Mahratta invasions. The glory of the temple is its corridors or open galleries. They extend to a total length of nearly 4,000 feet. Their breadth varies from 20 feet to 30 feet, and their height is about 30 feet. Some stones 40 feet long are used in doorways and roofs.

The temple was probably built during the 17th century, when the Ramnad Rajas were at the height of their independence and prosperity, and when their master, Tirumala Nayak, was erecting buildings in the same style at Madura.

The *lingam* is supposed to have been placed here by Rama. It is washed with Ganges water, which is afterwards sold.

Tinnevelly, properly *Tirunelvéli*, 'the sacred rice field,' occupies the extreme south-eastern corner of the Indian Peninsula. The Ghats, represented in the picture, divide it from Travancore. It is generally a sandy plain, with clumps of palmyra palms; but along the banks of the rivers, rice fields, with a variety of trees and crops render the country more pleasing. The district is noted for the number of its Christians. *Srivilliputur*, also called *Nachiyarkoil*, is a town containing about 20,000 inhabitants. The annual Car festival is attended by about 10,000 people.

SIKH TEMPLES.

Before describing the Amritsar temple, a short account may be given of the Sikhs and their doctrines.

The word *Sikh*, corrupted from *Sishya*, means disciple, one who is to be instructed. It is used to express the close dependence of the sect on their Gurus. Nanak, the founder, was born near Lahore in the year 1469. The lives of him, called *Janan-sakhis*, are filled with wonderful stories. "It is said that all the Hindu gods appeared in the sky and announced the birth of Bhagat, a great saint, to save the world. He travelled a great deal. It is said that he could fly through the air, and if he did not wish to go to a place, he could make it come to him. He performed the pilgrimage to Mecca. On being reproved from lying down with his feet towards the Kaaba, which was considered disrespectful, Nanak inquired in which direction he could turn his feet when the same disrespect would not be offered, for God is everywhere.

THE GOLDEN TEMPLE OF UMRITSUR.

Nanak's teaching was mainly based on that of Kabir, a Hindu reformer. His idea was to bring about a union between Hindus and Muhammadans, on the common ground of a belief in one God. Yet the creed of Nanak was really more pantheistic (that all is God) than monotheistic (that there is only one God). God, he said, is the Supreme Lord, Paramesvara. He may be called Brahma, or by other names, such as Govinda, etc., but his especial name is Hari. This Supreme Being does not create the universe out of nothing, but evolves it out of himself for his own amusement (kheta). Such expansion is made up of the three Gunas—Sattva, Rajas and Tamas in perfect harmony. Except in denouncing idolatry, Nanak differed very little from a pure Vaishnava, for he taught that in the present Kali-Yuga the repetition of the name of Hari is the only means of salvation from the misery of successive births, and that the knowledge of this name is only to be acquired through a proper Guru. It is curious that a religious movement intended to draw the Sikhs and Muhammadans together should have ended in exciting the bitterest animosity between them.

Nanak died in 1538. One of his sons expected to succeed him, but he nominated as second guru, his disciple Lahana. He was quite illiterate, although tradition makes him inventor of the alphabet called Guru-mukhi (a modification of the Devanagari), in which the Sikh scriptures were written. Lahana, whose name had been changed to Angada, nominated Amardas to succeed him as third guru. The other chief gurus were 4. Ram-das ; 5. Arjun ; 6. Har-Govind ; 7. Har-Rai ; 8. Har-Kisan (for Har-Krishna) ; 9. Teg-Bahadur ; and 10. Govind Sinh.

TOWER OF BABA ATAL, AMRITSAR, BUILT OVER THE TOMB OF A SON OF THE FOURTH GURU, HAR-GOVIND.

Ram-das conveyed his precepts to his followers in the form of verses. Many of his stanzas, together with the sayings of the previous gurus, were collected by Arjun who gave the Sikhs their first bible, called the Granth or book (Sanskrit Grantha). Arjun was the first guru who aimed at temporal as well as spiritual power. This excited the suspicions of the Muhammadans, and Arjun's death is said to have been brought about by the Emperor Jahangir.

Aurangzeb tortured Teg-Bahadur, the 9th guru, so cruelly that he induced a fellow prisoner to put an end to his sufferings. But the murder changed the Sikhs into a nation of fighting men. Teg-Bahadur's son, Govind Sinh, the tenth guru, formed the design of establishing an independent dominion on the ruins of the Muhammadan Empire. He abolished caste among his followers, as disunion would have been a source of weakness. They were to add Sinh to their other names. They were to be distinguished by long hair; they were always to carry a sword—in token of engaging in perpetual warfare with Muhammadans; and to wear short trousers. No animal was to be eaten unless killed by a Sikh, and no beef was to be touched. The Sikh was never to wear a cap, nor to shave his head or beard; nor to take off his turban while eating.

Govind composed a second Granth, called the book of the Tenth Guru. He substituted war for peace as a religious duty. Thenceforward the Sikhs were to imitate the Muhammadans—they were to spread their religion, not by persuasion, but by the sword. They were even to worship the sword. The greater part of Govind's life was spent in war, and at last he was assassinated. There is a temple at Patna, where he was brought up, dedicated to him.

Govind refused to appoint a successor, saying, "After me you shall everywhere mind the book of the Granth Sahib as your Guru; whatever you shall ask, it will show you." The *Adi-Granth* (Original Records), was translated into English a few years ago by Professor Triumpp. He considers it "an extremely incoherent and wearisome book, the few thoughts and ideas it contains being repeated in endless varieties." "It is a jumbling together of metrical precepts and apophthegms, supposed to have been composed by at least 35 different authors, among whom are 10 professional panegyrists, employed to write eulogies on the Guru."

The Sikhs observe caste, and in most respects conform to the customs of the Hindus. They even surpass the ordinary Hindu in some of his most inveterate superstitions; as, for example, in ascribing divine sanctity to the cow. At one time in the Punjab, it was infinitely more criminal to kill a cow than to kill a daughter, meriting nothing less than capital punishment. This arose simply from opposition to the Musalmans, who, whenever they conquered a district peopled by Hindus, invariably slaughtered cows, both to ratify their victories, and to show their contempt for Hindu superstitions. The Sikhs, when it was in their power, retaliated by killing pigs in mosques.

A SIKH.

Sikhs may drink wine, but they must refrain from tobacco. Its use would destroy all the merit previously acquired.

There is a class of Sikh fanatics, called *Akalis*, worshippers of the timeless God. They wear a high-peaked turban, encircled by steel *chakras*, used as weapons. They believe themselves justified in putting to death every opponent of their religion.

The Sikhs number about 18 lakhs. They were the most gallant foes the English ever encountered in India; but they are now very loyal to the British Government, and during the Mutiny they rendered most essential service.

AMRITSAR, the sacred city of the Sikhs, is about 32 miles from Lahore, the capital of the Punjab. It was commenced by Ramdas, the 4th guru, on a site granted by the

Emperor Akbar. He also excavated the holy tank from which the city derives its name, 'pool of immortality,' and in its midst began to erect a temple which was completed by his son. In 1762, Ahmed Shah, the Afghan, completely routed the Sikhs. He destroyed the town of Amritsar, blew up the temple with gunpowder, filled the sacred tank with mud, and defiled the holy place by the slaughter of cows. After a while, the desecrated shrine was restored. In 1802, Ranjit Singh seized Amritsar. He spent large sums of money upon the great shrine, and roofed it with sheets of copper gilt, whence the building derives its popular name of the Golden Temple. It is also called Hari-Mandira, or sometimes Durbar Sahib. It stands in the centre of a large square tank, bordered by a marble pavement and is approached by a marble causeway. All the lower part is of marble, inlaid with precious stones, and here and there overlaid with gold and silver. The interior is even more gorgeous than the exterior. On the grand floor is a vaulted hall—its richly gilded ceiling ornamented with an infinite number of small mirrors, and its walls decorated with inlaid work of various designs, flowers, birds, and elephants. Four short passages, entered by carved silver doors, one on each of its 4 sides, lead to this vaulted chamber. In the interior, opposite the principal entrance, sits the presiding Guru—his legs folded under him, with the open Granth before him. He is attended by other officials of the temple, who assist him in chanting the sacred texts.

A GURU READING THE GRANTHA.

The Brahmans maintain that God may infuse his essence into images, but never make an idol of the written Veda; Sikhism, on the contrary, denies that God associates Himself with images, but believe that He is manifested in the Granth. Every morning it is dressed out in costly brocade, and reverently placed on a low throne under a jewelled canopy. All day long chowries are waved over the sacred volume, and every evening, it is transported to the sacred temple on the edge of the lake opposite the causeway, where it is made to repose for the night in a golden bed within a consecrated chamber.

A constant line of worshippers, male and female, enter the temple one after the other, cast down their offerings, and bow their heads to the ground before the Granth and the Guru.

Sir Monier Williams says: "On leaving the temple I talked for a time with an intelligent Sikh who had received an English education. Pointing to an idol of Krishna which had been set up in the margin of the lake, I asked whether the Sikhs were returning to the worship of Vaishnava images. "Yes," he said, "we are gradually lapsing back into our old habits. Our first Guru abolished caste and forbade the worship of idols. Our tenth Guru was a thorough Hindu at heart, and by his own example encouraged the return to Hindu practices; so that of the Sikhs now found in the Punjab a large number adopt caste, wear the Brahmanical thread, keep Hindu festivals, observe Hindu ceremonies (such as the Shraddha), and even present offerings to idols in Hindu temples."

Sir Monier Williams visited the temple at Patna, dedicated to the tenth Guru. Its guardian was an Akali. In a small recess were some of the Guru's garments, and what was once his bed, all in a state of decay. On a low altar was a beautiful copy of the Granth. In the centre, on a raised platform, were numerous sacred swords, which appeared to be as much objects of worship as the sacred books.*

* The whole of this section is abridged from *Brahmanism and Hinduism*, by Sir Monier Williams, Murray, Publisher.

JAIN TEMPLES.

Jainism.—Some account may be given of this system before describing its temples.

The name is derived from ***Jina***, 'Conqueror,' applied to the 24 saints, who are also called *Tirthamkaras*, 'ford-makers,' making a ford across the troubled sea of transmigrations to Nirvana. The system very much resembles Buddhism, which will afterwards be described. Both originated from Hinduism, Jainism probably somewhat earlier.

The Jains, like Buddhists, deny the existence of a great Creator, and hold in the highest esteem certain teachers. They distinguish the 24 Jinas of the present age from each other in colour, stature, and longevity. ***Rishabha***, the first Jina, was 500 poles in height, and lived 8,400,000 years. The age of his successor declined to 7,200,000 years, his height to 450 poles. The downward movement thus continued throughout the following generations. The last two Tirthamkaras, Parsvanath and Mahavira, were human as regard their life and their size. The last is supposed to have lived about the same time as Buddha.

The Jain legends about the birth and life of Mahavira very much resemble those about Buddha. His father, Siddhartha, was the chief of the village of Kundagrama; his mother, Trisala, was sister of Ketaka, king of Vaisali. On the night of his birth, the celestial ones, descending and ascending, shed a divine lustre over the universe, and the conflux of the gods caused great confusion and noise. Mahavira remained in his home till his 29th year, when he left his silver and gold, and distributed presents amongst the poor. He went to the jungle and was houseless; he plucked out his hair in five handfuls; after a year, he abandoned the use of clothes, and went naked in the wilderness. After 12 years he became a perfect saint. He lived afterwards for 30 years, going about from place to place. In the 42nd year of his renunciation, in the 30th year of his 'knowledge,' and in the 72nd year of his life, he breathed his last. Buddha became a conqueror through profound meditation; whereas Mahavira was a Jina through severe bodily austerity.

The Jains are divided into two principal sects. They had a notion that a sense of shame implied sin, so that if there were no sin in the world, there would be no shame. Hence they argued illogically that to get rid of clothes was to get rid of sin; and every ascetic who aimed at sinlessness was enjoined to walk about naked, with the sky (Dig) as his sole covering (*Dig-ambara*).

In process of time a sect arose opposed to the above practice. They called themselves *Svetambaras*, that is, 'clothed in white garments.' The separation is supposed to have taken place some time before the first century of the Christian era. The Svetambaras object to images of any of the Jinas entirely naked. Hence all Svetambara statues ought to have some appearance of a line round the middle of the body, representing a strip of cloth. The Svetambaras admit women into their order of ascetics; whereas the Digambaras, for obvious reasons, do not. At present the Digambaras wear coloured garments, and confine the disuse of clothes only to their meals.

The Jains are divided into *Yatis* and *Sravakas*, religious and lay orders. The Yati has to lead a life of continence; he should wear a thin cloth over his mouth to prevent insects from flying into it, and he should carry a broom to sweep the place on which he is about to sit, to remove every living creature out of the way of danger; but, in turn, he may dispense with all acts of worship. The *Sravaka* has to add to the observance of the religious and moral duties the worship of the saints, and a profound reverence for his more pious brethren. He must practise the four virtues—liberality, gentleness, piety, and penance; he must abstain at certain seasons from salt, flowers, green fruits, roots, honey, grapes, tobacco; drink water thrice strained, and never leave a liquid uncovered, lest an insect should be drowned in it. It is his duty also daily to visit a temple where some of the images of the Jain saints are placed, walk round it three times, make an obeisance to the image, and make some offerings of fruits or flowers. The reader in a Jain temple is a Yati, but the ministrant priest is not seldom a Brahman, since the Jains have no priests of their own.

The Jains have no dagabas for preserving the relics of their saints. They believe in separate individual souls, whereas Buddhists deny the existence of souls. Souls, according to the Jains, may exist in stocks, stones, lumps of earth, drops of water, particles of fire, &c.

The Jaina 'three jewels' are Right-belief, Right-knowledge, and Right-conduct, whereas the Buddhist Tri-ratna consists in Buddha, the Law, and the Monkhood. The fifth Jain precept is, "Have no worldly attachments," whereas with Buddhists it is "Drink no strong

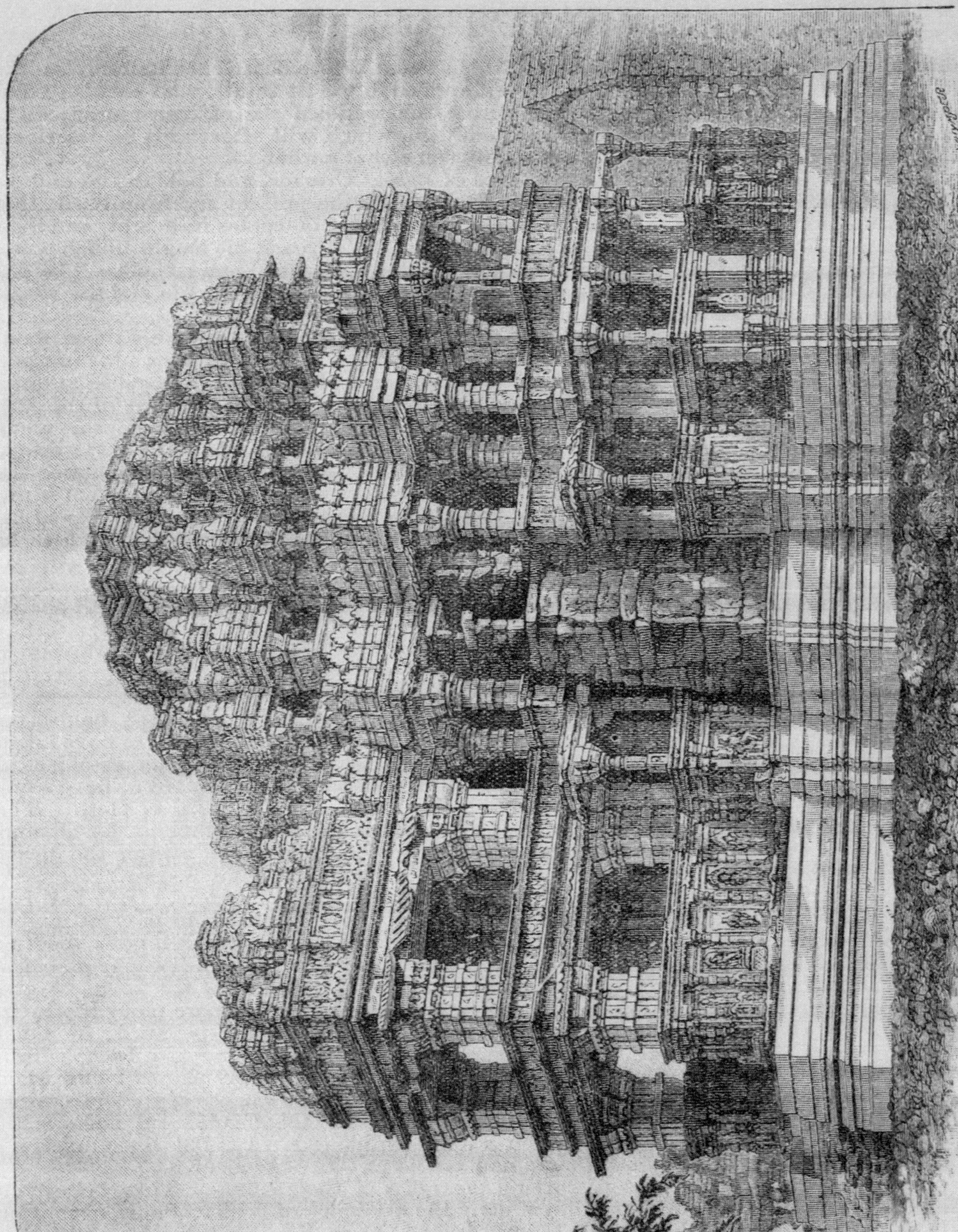

SAS BAHU JAIN TEMPLE, GWALIOR.

drink." The Jains lay even more stress than the Buddhists on the first prohibition:—Kill no living creature.

The prayer formula of the Jains differs from the three Refuges of the Buddhists. It is "Reverence to the Arhats, to the Siddhas, to the Acharyas, to the Upadhyayas, to all the Saddhus.*

Jainism, Sir Monier Williams thinks, is gradually drifting back into the current of Brahmanism which everywhere surrounds it and attracts it. In 1891 the Jains numbered 1,416,638, found chiefly in Rajputana and Western India.

The mercy of the Jains is very much limited to the lower animals. They will feed ants, pigeons, &c.; but many of them are merciless oppressors of the victims who fall into their hands as debtors. In Kathiawar they strongly opposed the slaughter of cattle, but they had not a word to say against female infanticide.

A few of the principal Jain temples will now be described.

Parasnath, about 200 miles north-west from Calcutta, is the sacred Jain mountain in Bengal. It stands clear out of the plain, and is a narrow rocky ridge, the topmost peak of which is 4,488 feet above the sea. The summit, called by the Jains *Asmid Sikhar*, 'The Peak of Bliss,' is composed of a small table-land, flanked by 20 small Jain temples on the craggy peaks.

The Jains assert that 10 of their 24 Tirthamkaras attained Nirwana on this sacred mountain, which is called after Parswa, the 23rd. Nineteen Tirthamkaras are said to be buried here. The temples are either modern or old ones restored. Some of them are very beautiful, especially a little shrine of white marble, which cost Rs. 80,000.

Sas Bahu Temple, Gwalior.—Gwalior has already been described (see page 26). The Sas Bahu temple is said to be dedicated to Padmanabha, the sixth Tirthamkara. It is supposed to have been erected about A. D. 1093. All that remains standing is the cruciform porch, measuring 100 feet in length, and 63 feet across the arms. Of the rest of the building, only the foundation remains. The porch, which is 3 storeys in height, is, on the whole, in fair preservation, but the roof is much shattered. The surface is covered with sculptures of human beings, animals, flowers, and ornaments. The central hall is 30 feet square, with 4 large pillars bearing its great pyramidal roof, which is elaborately decorated.

The most striking Jain work at Gwalior, are the rock-cut sculptures, excavated all round the face of the cliff, about 100 in all, varying in size from a huge colossus 57 feet high, to ordinary life-size figures. Eighteen of them are over 20 feet high. Most of them are representations of Adinath, the first Tirthamkara. They are known by his symbol on the pedestal, a bull. A seated figure of Neminath, the 22nd Tirthamkara, is 30 feet high, his symbol being a shell. They were all excavated during the 33 years from A. D. 1441—74.

Abu.—Abu is a celebrated mountain in the south of Rajputana, rising like a large granite island from the plain. The summit is an undulating plateau, broken by fantastic peaks, the topmost point being 5,650 feet above the sea. In the midst of the plateau is a beautiful lake, called the Nail Lake, because it is said to have been excavated by the nails of the gods to protect themselves from the Asur Mahik!

Abu has the most beautiful Jain temples in India. They are at *Deulwara*, the 'place of temples', about a mile from the station. There are 5 temples in all, one of the largest being three-storeyed, and dedicated to Rishaba. The shrine has 4 doors facing the 4 cardinal points. The image inside is quadruple and is called a *Chaumukh*.

To the west of the *Chaumukh* stand the two finest temples of Abu, the one known as Vimalasah's, dedicated to Adinatha, another name of Rishaba; and opposite to it on the north side, the temple of Vastupala and Tejahpala, dedicated to Neminath, the 22nd Tirthamkara. Both temples are built of white marble, brought from a distance of 300 miles, and dragged up to the top of this steep mountain. They are also carved with all the delicacy and richness of ornament which the resources of Indian art at the time of their erection could devise. Inscriptions fix the date of the Vimalasah temple at 1031 A.D., and the construction of the Vastupal edifice from 1197 to 1247.

The temple of Vimalasah consists of a shrine lighted only from the door, containing a cross-legged seated figure in brass of Rishaba, to whom this temple is dedicated. In front of this is a platform, which, with the shrine, is raised 2 steps above the surrounding court. The platform and greater part of the court are covered by a *mandap*, or outer portico, shaped

* Chiefly from *Buddhism*, by Sir M. Williams, Murray, Publisher.

JAIN TEMPLE, ABU, IMAGE OF RISHABHA, THE FIRST TIRTHAMKARA.

like a cross, and supported by 48 columns. The 8 central pillars are so arranged as to form an octagon, supporting a dome, which, together with its circular rims and richly carved pendant, forms the most striking and beautiful feature of the entire composition. The whole is enclosed in an oblong courtyard, about 140 feet by 90 feet, surrounded by 55 cells, each of which contains a cross-legged statue of one or other of the Tirthamkaras. The door posts and lintels of the cells are carved in most elaborate devices, with human figures interspersed with foliage and architectural ornaments of the most varied complexity. In a small cell in the south-west corner is the image of the devi Ambaji.

Facing the entrance to the temple is a square building containing 9 white marble elephants, on each of which is a male figure, although some have been broken away. This represents Vimalasah and his family going in procession to the temple. Vimalasah is represented by a clay figure on horseback, the original statue having been destroyed by some Moslem.

In Vastupala's temple a procession similar to this, with an elaborately carved spire, occupies the place of the cells behind the shrine in that of Vimalasah. It is separated from the court by a pierced screen of open tracery. Behind it are 10 elephants of very exquisite workmanship, and with rich trappings sculptured with the most exquisite precision. The riders, however, have been carried off. In this case the loss is not so great, for behind each elephant is a niche containing statues of those who were, or were to be, mounted on them. These are Vastupala with his one wife ; Tejahpala, with two ; and their uncle seems to have had three. The men, says Fergusson, are "fine looking fellows, all with flowing beards ; the ladies are generally sharp-visaged, sour-looking dames."

Vimalasah was a merchant ; the brothers Vastupala and Tejahpala were bankers of Anahilapattan, who served as chief ministers to Vira Dhavala, the first of the Waghela dynasty of Gujarat.

Palitana.—Palitana is situated on the east of the Kathiawar Peninsula, and is the chief town of the Palitana State. It lies at the eastern base of the Satrunjaya Hill, considered the holiest of the 5 Jain sacred mountains. The other four are Girnar, Abu, Parasnath, and Gwalior.

Satrunjaya hill is nearly 2,000 feet above sea-level. The summit is divided into two peaks, but the valley between them has been partly built over by a wealthy Jain merchant. The entire summit is covered with temples, among which the most famous are those of Adinath, Kumar Pal, Vimalasah, Sampriti Raja, and Chaumukh. The last is the most lofty, and can be clearly distinguished at a distance of 25 miles. The Jains consider the mountain "The first of all places of pilgrimages, the bridal hall of those who would win everlasting rest." There is hardly a city in India that has not at one time or other contributed to erect the edifices which crown the hill. Street after street, square after square, extend these shrines of the Jain faith, with their stately enclosures, half palace, half fortress, raised in marble magnificence upon the lonely and majestic mountain.

At the foot of the ascent there are many little cells, with a marble slab carved into the representation of the soles of two feet (*charan*), very flat ones, and generally with the toes all of one length. They are very numerous all the way up the hill. Jains unable to afford the expense of a complete temple erect these cells. The path is paved with rough stones all the way up, with here and there flights of steps. High up there is a small temple of Hanuman, the image bedaubed with vermilion. Higher up still, is the shrine of a Musalman *pir*. From the top of the mountain, there is a magnificent view.

The hill is a city of temples. Except a few tanks, there is nothing else within the gates. The silence, too, is striking. Now and then in the mornings you hear a bell for a few seconds, or the beating of a drum for a short time, and on holidays chants from the larger temples meet your ear ; but generally during the after-part of the day the only sounds are those of vast flocks of pigeons that rush about from the roof of one temple to that of another. Parroquets and squirrels, doves and ringdoves abound, and peacocks are occasionally met on the outer walls. Each temple enclosure is protected by strong gates and walls, and all gates are carefully closed at sun-down.

In the temple of Chaumukh there are 4 large white marble figures of Adinath, each facing one of the 4 doors of the shrine. They sit with their feet crossed in front, their heads rising about 10 feet above the pedestal. The aspect of these, and of all the images is peculiar. Frequently on the brow and middle of the breast there is a diamond, set in silver or gold, and almost always the breasts are mounted with one of the precious metals, whilst there are occasionally gold plates on the shoulders, elbow and knee-joints and a crown on the head. But the peculiar feature is the eyes, which seem to peer at you like so many cats. They seem to be made of silver, overlaid with pieces of glass, very clumsily cemented on, and in every case projecting so far and of such a form, as to give one the idea of their wearing spectacles over eyes in diseased sockets.

The Jains build temples as a work of merit without any reference to their use. On the Satrunjaya Hill a few *Yatis* or priests sleep in the temples, and perform the daily services, and a few attendants are constantly there to keep the place clean or to feed the sacred pigeons, but there are no human habitations properly so called. The pilgrim ascends in the morning, and returns when he has performed his devotions. He must not eat, or at least he must not cook his food, on the sacred hill, and he must not sleep there. It is a city of the gods, and meant for them only.

Most of the temples are modern.

Girnar, next in sanctity to Satrunjaya, lies to the westward in Kathiawar, 10 miles east of Junagarh town. The hill rises about 3,500 feet above sea-level. A rock at the foot of the hill outside the town is covered with Asoka's inscriptions, 250 B.C.

There are six rest houses on the ascent to the temple of Neminath. The temple of Ambamata, which crowns the first peak of the hill, is much resorted to by newly married couples of the different sub-divisions of Brahmans. The bride and bridegroom have their clothes tied together, and attended by their male and female relations, present cocoanuts and other offerings to the goddess whose favour is sought to secure a continuance of wedded happiness.

The principal group of temples at Girnar, about 16 in number, is situated on a ledge about 600 feet from the summit. The largest, and possibly the oldest of them, is that of Neminath. An inscription upon it records that it was repaired in A.D. 1278. The temple stands in a courtyard, measuring 195 feet by 130 over all. Around the courtyard are arranged 70 cells, with a covered and enclosed passage in front of them, each of which contains a cross-legged seated figure of Neminath, and generally with a sculpture or picture representing some event in his life. Immediately behind the temple of Neminath is a triple one erected by the brothers Tejahpala and Vastupala, who also erected one of the principal temples in Abu.

The Jains were once numerous in South India. Many images of their Tirthamkaras have been dug up. Some are to be found in the Madras Museum. A severe persecution by a Saiva prince of the Pandyan country reduced their numbers. On the wall of the holy tank enclosure fronting the shrine of Minakshi in the great temple at Madura, there is a representation of a long line of Jains impaled, with dogs licking the trickling blood, and crows flying around to pick out their eyes.

BUDDHIST TEMPLES AND BUILDINGS.

Introduction.

Before describing a few of the principal Buddhist temples, some account may be given of the founder of the religion.

The word Buddha comes from *budh*, to know. Gautama, the founder of Buddhism, claimed to be *sarvagnya*, omniscient, or to know all things. The religion which he established has many followers in Ceylon and Eastern Asia.

Birth.—The time when Buddha lived is somewhat uncertain. Twenty different dates have been given. In Ceylon he is supposed to have died 543 years before the Christian era. As he is said to have lived 80 years, he must have been born about 623 B.C.; but probably it was 60 years or more later.

The birth-place of Gautama was Kapilavastu, a town about 100 miles north of Benares. His father, Suddhodana, (one possessed of pure rice) was ruler of the Sakya tribe. Hence Gautama was sometimes called Sakya Muni. His mother, Maya, was childless till her 45th year.

Most wonderful stories are told of the birth of Buddha. According to the Burmese account, Bodhisat,* a candidate for Buddhahood, entered her womb in the form of a white elephant, and was seen there like a white thread, passed through the finest pearls. Sinhalese books say that he could be seen like a priest seated on a throne preaching. At his birth he took seven steps forward, a lotus springing up at each step, and said with a loud voice, "I am the most exalted in the world, I am the chief of the world; hereafter there is to me no other birth." These words, which rolled to the highest Brahma-lókas, made the gods assemble to do homage to the new-born prince. The 10,000 Sakwalas trembled; flowers were showered from the sky—even the whole surface of the ocean was covered with them.

On the fifth day he was called Siddhartha (Pali, Siddhattha), "he who has accomplished his aim." His family name was Gautama (Pali, Gotamo). The Brahmans predicted that he

* Called in Burmese, *Phralong*.

would forsake the world to become a Buddha after seeing four omens—namely a man worn-out with age, a sick man, a dead body, and an ascetic. From that time his father took all possible means to prevent his seeing any of these things: no sign of sorrow or pain was allowed to come near him.

Early Life.—Gautama's mother died in a week. Mahapajapati, her sister, became his foster-mother. In his 16th year he was married to Yasodhara, daughter of the king of Koli. Besides her, he is said to have had 40,000 concubines and singing women. Till his 29th year, Siddhartha lived in the full enjoyment of every kind of pleasure. One day when the prince, with a large retinue, was driving through the eastern gate of the city on the way to one of his parks, he met on the road a deva, who appeared as an old man, broken and decrepit. He was bent on his stick, and all his limbs and joints trembled. "Who is that man?" said the prince to his charioteer. "He is small and weak: his body is wasted away; leaning on his stick, he is hardly able to walk, stumbling at every step. Is there something peculiar in his family, or is that the common lot of all beings?" "Sir," replied the charioteer, "that man is sinking under old age, his senses have become obtuse, and suffering has destroyed his strength. But that is not peculiar to his family. Your father, your mother, all your relations, all your friends, will come to the same state; this is the appointed end of all creatures."

"Alas!" replied the prince, "are creatures so ignorant, so weak and foolish, as to be proud of the youth by which they are intoxicated, not seeing the old age which awaits them? As for me, I go away. Turn my chariot quickly. What have I, the future prey of old age,—what have I to do with pleasure?" And the prince returned to the city without going to his park.

Another time the prince was driving through the southern gate to his pleasure garden, when the same deva appeared like a man parched with fever, his body twisted, without a friend, hardly able to breathe, and frightened at the approach of death. Having questioned his charioteer, and received from him the answer which he expected, the young prince said, "Alas! health is but the sport of a dream, and the fear of suffering must take this frightful form. Where is the wise man, who, after having seen what he is, could any longer think of joy and pleasure?" The prince turned his chariot and returned to the city.

A third time he was driving to his pleasure garden through the western gate. The deva assumed the appearance of a dead body on the road, with worms issuing from the nine apertures. Upon the sight of this, the prince, again calling to his charioteer to witness it, exclaimed, "Oh! woe to youth which must be destroyed by old age! Woe to health, which must be destroyed by so many diseases! Woe to this life, where a man remains so short a time! If there was no old age, no disease, no death; if these could be made captive for ever!" The prince then said, "Let us turn back, I must think how to accomplish deliverance."

Lastly, Siddhartha saw on the same road the deva, appearing as a mendicant, clad in a becoming manner, not looking farther before him than the distance of a yoke, and showing much inward peace. When informed by the charioteer whom it was that he saw, he learned with much satisfaction that by this means future births might be overcome, and ordered the charioteer to drive on towards the pleasure-garden.

Leaves Home.—The same day Yasodhara gave birth to a son, called Rahula; but that night the prince determined to give up every thing, that he might discover for himself and for the world the way of salvation from sorrow.

The prince commanded Channa, who was on guard, to get his horse Kantaka ready. Whilst he was absent in the stable, Siddhartha went to the apartment of Yasodhara, that he might see his son. On opening the door he saw her asleep with the child on her bosom also asleep. Lest she should awake, Siddhartha did not enter farther. He then mounted his horse and left at midnight. The devas opened the gate of the city that he might pass through, and 60,000 of them, with torches of jewels, went before him to light the way, while as many surrounded him on the right hand and on the left. The horse travelled 30 yojanas in one night, and at a single bound carried the prince and Channa over a river 800 cubits in breadth. Siddhartha, at this place, gave his ornaments and Kantaka to Channa, requesting him to go back and tell his father and wife that he had become an ascetic. Afterwards the prince cut off his hair with his sword, and exchanged his dress with a peasant.

Seeks Buddhahood.—Siddhartha first went to Vesali and became a pupil of Alara, a famous Brahman; but having learned all that he could teach him, he went away disappointed : he had not found the road to salvation. He next tried Uddaka, another Brahman at Rajagaha, the capital of Magadha. There, too, he looked in vain for the means of deliverance from the miseries of life.

Gautama afterwards went to the Uruvela forest, where he was joined by five Brahmans. For six years he gave himself to the most severe penances. At last he became so weak that he fell senseless to the ground, and was supposed to be dead. On recovering, he thought that asceticism was not the way of arriving at the truth. "If," he said "abstention from sufficient food is meritorious, the wild beasts, who are content with grass, ought to abound in merit." To regain his strength, Gautama again went from place to place with the alms bowl and partook of food. His Brahman companions then forsook him, and went to Benares.

Conflict with Mara.—Wasawartti Mára,* ruler of the sixth déva-lóka, considering that if Gautama became Buddha he would lose his influence, followed him from Kapilavastu, constantly trying to seduce him from his purpose. The last attempt was made while Gautama sat under the bo-tree in Uruvela, determined not to leave it till he had attained complete knowledge. It is thus described :

When Mára saw that the Bodhisat had taken this resolution, he came into his presence riding on an elephant 2,400 miles high, appearing as a monster with 500 heads, 1,000 red eyes, and 500 flaming tongues ; he had also a thousand arms, in each of which was a weapon, no two of these weapons alike. With him also came an army of hideous demons, so large that it extended on every side 164 miles, and 9 miles upwards, while its weight was sufficient to overpoise the earth.

First Mára sent against the Bodhisat a terrific wind, which tore up the largest mountains ; then a rain storm, every drop the size of a palm tree ; then a shower of burning rocks and mountains ; then a shower of swords and spears, and all manner of sharp weapons ; then another of burning ashes ; then another of burning sand, and another of burning filth ; and then a fourfold darkness. But the wind moved him not ; the rain only refreshed him ; the burning mountains became garlands of flowers ; the weapons a shower of blossoms ; the burning coals, rubies ; the fiery ashes, fragrant sandal powder ; the burning sand, a shower of pearls ; and the darkness, a resplendent light.

Then came the whole army of Mára with himself at its head ; but their combined assault did not move him. Next Mára himself, in a form of frightful terror, cried with an awful voice, "Begone, from my throne." But the Bodhisat trembled not, "For," said he, "to gain this throne have I practised the ten virtues through more than four asankyas."† Then he recounted the alms he had given in a single birth, and called upon the earth to bear him witness ; and the earth responded with an awful roar, "I am witness to thee of that." Afterwards the earth opened, mountains of fire rose from the 136 hells, and the army of Màra fled discomfited. Then the three daughters of Màra, transforming themselves into beautiful maidens, and going to the tree where the Bodhisat remained sitting, sought in every way to seduce him from his resolution. After a long trial, they utterly failed, and went away.

Attainment of Buddhahood.—The conflict was now ended. Gautama acquired in the first watch of the night Knowledge of the Past ; in the middle watch Knowledge of the Present, and in the third watch the Knowledge of the Chain of Causation which leads to the Origin of Evil. Then he sang the song of triumph :—

"Through countless births have I wandered, seeking but not discovering the maker of this my mortal dwelling-house, and still again and again have birth and life and pain returned. But now at length art thou discovered, thou builder of this house. No longer shalt thou rear a house for me. Rafters and beams are shattered, and with destruction of Desire (*tanha*) deliverance from repeated life is gained at last."

Begins Preaching.—Before Buddha began his first sermon, Maha Meru‡ leaped with joy ; and the seven circles of rocks did obeisance to him. To hear the discourse, the déva-lokas were left empty, and the crowd was so great that a lakh of devas had no more space than the point of a needle. Though Buddha spoke in the language of Magadha, each one thought he spoke in his own tongue. At the conclusion, the oldest of the Brahmans and asankyas of devas entered the paths.

Buddha's Ministry.—While Gautama was near Benares, he was joined by a rich man, whose son, Yasa, was his first lay disciple. The father was the second. Yasa received *upasampada* ordination. The mother and former wife of Yasa were the first women who

* Called "*Man Nat*" by Bp. Bigandet. † A number inconceivably great. ‡ Burmese, *Mienmo*.

became lay disciples. Five mouths after his battle with Mára, Buddha's followers numbered about sixty persons. He then sent them out in different directions to preach and teach, Yasa only remaining at Benares near his parents.

"Go ye out, oh disciples," said he, "and travel from place to place, for the welfare of many people, for the joy of many people, in pity for the world, for the blessed welfare of gods and men."

Throughout his public life, Gautama was in the habit of travelling about most of the fine part of the year, preaching to the people; but during the rainy months in North India, from June to October, he remained in one place, devoting himself more particularly to the instruction of his disciples. This period, called *was* (from the Sanskrit *varsha* rain,) is in Ceylon a fine part of the year; but it is held at the same time, although the seasons differ. The people then assemble at night, both for amusement and in the hope of obtaining merit for themselves by hearing *bana*.

Unlike the Brahmans, Gautama admitted into the priesthood persons of all castes. His followers led an easy life, and were generally treated with respect. In course of time, he gained a large number of adherents. He was joined at once by a thousand fire-worshippers, disciples of Kasyapa and his two brothers. Two ascetics, named Sariputra and Moggalana, afterwards received, became leading members of the *Sangha*, or Society.

Death of Buddha.—The following account of Gautama's last day is abridged from the *Maha-parinibbana Suttanta*, "The Book of the Great Decease."

Gautama went about preaching for 45 years. At the end of that period, during *was*, he was attacked by a severe and painful illness. He recovered for a time, but felt that he could not live long.

"O Ananda," said he, "I am now grown old and full of years, my journey is drawing to its close. I am turning eighty years of age; and just as a worn-out cart, Ananda, can only with much additional care be made to move along, so, methinks, the body of the Tathágata can only be kept going with some additional care."

His followers were to depend upon themselves alone:

"Therefore, O Ananda, be ye lamps unto yourselves. Hold fast to the truth as a lamp. Look not for refuge to any one besides yourselves."

Afterwards Gautama asked Ananda to assemble his disciples in the neighbourhood of Vesali. When they met he said:

"The final extinction of the Tathágata will take place before long. At the end of three months from this time, the Tathágata will die."

At Pává, Chunda, a smith, prepared a meal of rice, cakes, and pork for Buddha and his disciples. Buddha alone ate the pork; the rice and sweet cakes being given to those with him. The pork that remained was buried in a hole. Soon afterwards the pork caused a severe attack of dysentery. When he was a little relieved, he said to Ananda, "Come, let us go to Kusinara." When he had gone some distance he went aside to the foot of a tree and said, "Fold, I pray you, Ananda, the robe, and spread it out for me. I am weary, and must rest a while." When Buddha was seated he said, "Fetch me, I pray you, Ananda, some water. I am thirsty, and would drink." Afterwards he bathed in the river, and went on his journey; but when he came to the mango grove he was again weary and had to lie down. When he had rested, he went with a great company to a grove of sal trees. There he lay down on a couch between two trees, never to rise again.

Ananda went aside weeping. Buddha called for him and said, "Do not weep: have I not already, on former occasions, told you that it is in the very nature of all things most near and dear unto us that we must divide ourselves from them, leave them. You have done well, Ananda! Be earnest in effort, and you too shall soon be free from the great evils." His last words to his followers were:

"Behold, now brethren, I exhort you saying, Decay is inherent in all component things. Work out, with diligence, your own perfection." Shortly afterwards he became unconscious, and in that state passed away.

A grand funeral pile was prepared by the Mallas of Kusinara, but it would not burn till Maha Kasyapa had come with 500 priests, and worshipped at the feet of Buddha. Then the funeral pile caught fire of itself. When the body was consumed, torrents of water from above and beneath extinguished the flame. The bones that remained were taken with a grand procession to the city, where they were afterwards distributed.

BUDDHISM AFTER GAUTAMA'S DEATH.

Councils.—The First General Council was held near Rajagaha, in the season of *was* following the death of Buddha. It consisted of 500 members under the Presidency of Maha Kasyapa. The place of meeting was a large cave, prepared for the occasion by the King of Magadha. Then the whole Council chanted together the words of Buddha, following Upali for the *Vinaya*, and Ananda for the *Dhamma*.

The Second Council met about 100 years after the First at Vesali. Seven hundred priests assembled. The object was to forbid certain departures from the rules laid down by Buddha; as, that food might be taken a little afternoon, that gold and silver might be received, &c. These practices were condemned, but the decisions of the Council were not universally acknowledged, and a separation took place. In course of time no less than 18 different Buddhist sects arose.

The Third Council was held at Pataliputra, now Patna, on the Ganges, during the reign of Asoka, king of Magadha. One thousand elders assembled for nine months, and once more the rules of the order and the doctrines were repeated and settled.

Spread of Buddhism.—Asoka, or Dharmmasoka, king of Magadha, was a zealous convert to Buddhism. He established hospitals for man and beast, he dug wells, and planted trees on the roadsides. He caused inscriptions, in which he calls himself Piyadasi, the delight of the gods, to be engraved on rocks and pillars from Bengal to the borders of Afghanistan, some of which exist to the present day.

Asoka erected dagabas* for the relics of Buddha, and built so many wiharas,† that a province of India is still called Behar, the land of wiharas. The influence of Asoka had a great effect in spreading Buddhism. For several centuries, Benares was a Buddhist city.

At the close of the Third Council, Buddhist missionaries were sent to different countries. Mahinda, son of Asoka, with six persons, was appointed to introduce Buddhism into Ceylon. It is said that they came instantaneously through the air, and alighted at Mihintalé, near Anuradhapura. Soon after, Mahinda met king Tissa, who was out hunting with 40,000 attendants, all of whom immediately embraced Buddhism. It is said that Mahinda's voice could be heard all over Ceylon. Mahinda was followed by his sister Sanghamitta, who brought a branch of the bo-tree, which was planted at Anuradhapura.

Afghanistan and the countries to the north of India received Buddhism from Benares, through Sanskrit books. Buddhist missionaries went to China about 70 years before Christ. From China, the religion was carried to Japan.

BUDDHIST TEMPLES AND REMAINS.

Before describing individual remains, a brief account may be given of the different classes of them.

STUPAS.—Stúpa, from a root meaning "to heap," "to erect," is applied to any pile or mound erected over any spot memorable in the history of Buddhism. Stúpa has been corrupted into the Anglo-Indian word "Tope."

DAGABAS.—This is supposed to be shortened from *dhatu*, a relic, and *garbha*, a shrine. It is a mound erected over any of the relics of Buddha or of distinguished monks. The general form is semicircular.

CHAITYA CAVES.—Like *stúpa*, the word *Chaitya* is derived from a root *chitá*, signifying "heap." The form resembled a dagaba. As Chaityas were an essential feature of temples for purposes of worship, they were therefore called Chaitya caves.

VIHARAS.—These were for the accommodation of Buddhist monks living together in communities. The earliest form seems to have been that of one or more cells, with a verandah in front. In many instances the cells were small; in others they consisted of two apartments.

Besides the above, STAMBHAS, or LATS, pillars were erected in front of temples, and ORNAMENTAL RAILS were erected around stúpas, sacred trees and temples.

IMAGES OF BUDDHA.—Little sculpture was at first employed; but in later examples the pillars came to be elaborately carved. Though Buddha did not preach idol-worship, in

* Burmese, *Dzedis*. † Houses for priests; Burmese, *Kyoungs*.

course of time the plain dagaba ceased to satisfy the worshippers of certain sects, and the shrine came to be almost invariably occupied by an image of Buddha, seated on a sort of throne, called a *Sinhasana*, or "lion seat," because the ends of it rested on lions carved in low relief, and usually with an attendant on each hand bearing a fly-flap. Eventually this representation came to be repeated in all parts of the caves; while, in still later times, other beings were associated with him, first as attendants, and then as distinct objects of adoration. Such were the Indras, Bodhisattas, &c.*

BUDH-GAYA.

BUDH-GAYA is to the Buddhists the most sacred spot in the world. Under a pipal or bo-tree here, Gautama is supposed to have attained Buddhahood, after his terrible struggle with Mara.

As the temple has already been described, no further account of it is necessary, but the attempt of the Buddhists to recover possession of it may be noticed.

In 1894, Mr. H. Dharmapala, a Sinhalese, General Secretary of the Mahabodhi Society, presented a petition to the Government of Bengal, asking that Buddhist priests should be allowed to officiate three times a day in the temple, that Buddhists should be allowed to set up images, bells, flag-staffs, &c. The Mohant replied that they who had held the place for over 5 centuries were ready to meet all reasonable requirements of worshippers. Any well-grounded complaint that difficulties were imposed would meet with ready attention at the hands of the Bengal Government, but the Temple could not be transferred to Buddhists. It is possible, however, that some amicable arrangement may yet be made.

SARNATH.

SARNATH is next in sanctity to Budh-Gaya. Asoka is said to have erected a large *stúpa* on the spot, near Benares, where Buddha first taught his doctrines. It is a solid dome, 93 feet in diameter at the base, and 128 feet in height. The lower part is built of stone; the upper part of large bricks. The former has eight projecting faces, with niches to receive a statue. The eight statues have disappeared: they probably represented Buddha. The stones are held together by iron cramps. An ornamental band of geometric figures, flowers, and birds, goes round the middle of the lower portion. A low passage leads right through the *stúpa*. There is a small room in the centre, and a narrow opening to the top.

To the west of the tower are the remains of a hospital and of an old Buddhist monastery. Only the foundations are now visible.

The stúpa, or tower, is named *Dhamek*, probably a corruption of Dharma. The place is called *Sarnath*, probably a corruption of *Saranganath*, Lord of Deer. It was originally a deer garden.

There was another large brick *stúpa*, but it was demolished, for the sake of the bricks, by Jagat Singh, the Dewan of Raja Chait Singh of Benares.

About half a mile distant from the Dhamek stúpa there is a mound of solid brick work, 74 feet high. On the top there is an octagonal building, erected in 1531 A.D., to commemorate the ascent of the mound by the Emperor Humayun. This is now called Lori's Leap, from a Hindu, of the name of Lori, having leaped from its summit, and killed himself.

For several centuries Benares was the headquarters of Buddhism. The city then lay around Sarnath, to the north of the river Barna. After a time Hinduism began to recover its hold. The Brahmans adopted several Buddhist doctrines, and pretended that Vishnu appeared as Buddha to encourage wicked men to despise the Vedas, reject caste, and deny the existence of the gods to their own destruction. Hiuen Tsiang, a Chinese Buddhist pilgrim, visited India in the 7th century of the Christian era. He describes the people of Benares as "mostly unbelievers, a few reverence the law of Buddha. There are about 30 monasteries and 3,000 monks. There are a hundred or so Déva temples, with about 10,000 heretics. They honour principally Mahesvara. Some cut their hair off, others tie their hair in a knot, and go naked without clothes; they cover their bodies with ashes, and by the practice of all sorts of austerities, they seek to escape from transmigration."

---

* Abridged from *The Cave Temples of India*, by Fergusson and Burgess, pp. 171—177.

STUPA AT SARNATH, NEAR BENARES.

Sankar Acharya, who lived in the 8th or 9th century, by his disputations with the Buddhists and his writings, did much to promote the worship of Siva in Benares. In the eleventh or twelfth century, the Buddhists seem to have been finally expelled. Numbers of images concealed by the departing monks have been found buried near Sarnath, and heaps of ashes still lie scattered amidst the ruins to show that the monasteries were destroyed by fire. Major Kittoe, the Government Archæologist, who made extensive excavations at Sarnath, says: "All has been sacked and burned—priests, temples, idols, all together; for in some places bones, iron, wood and stone, are found in huge masses, and this has happened more than once."

Large numbers of statues have been dug out of the ruins, many of which are preserved in the grounds of the Government College.

BUDDHIST CAVE TEMPLES.

It is said that King Asoka, in the 3rd century B.C., was the first to excavate a cave for religious purposes. The oldest Buddhist cave temples now known are on the Phalgu river, about 16 miles north of Gaya. They are 7 in number, and not of great size. The largest is about 46 feet by 20. The earliest is said to have been excavated in the 12th year of Asoka, or B.C. 252. The latest dates from Asoka's grandson about 214 B.C.

Orissa Caves.—These are situated in a picturesque group of hills that rise out of the level plains of the delta of the Mahanadi, almost like islands from the ocean. They are composed of coarse sandstone rock, easily excavated. There is one of Asoka's inscriptions not far distant, and the Tooth Relic was brought to the neighbourhood immediately after the cremation of the body. There are about 16 excavations of importance in the Udayagiri hill, besides numerous little rock-cut cells in which a single ascetic could dwell. The excavations known popularly as the Rani Ka Nur, or the Queen's Palace, is the finest. It has two storeys, and occupies three sides of a square courtyard. The verandah in the upper storey is 63 feet long, and opens into 4 cells, each with 2 doors. The lower verandah is only 43 feet long, and opens into 3 cells. The walls are ornamented with sculptures.

WESTERN INDIA.

Behar was the cradle of Buddhism, and the first to adopt the cave form of architecture, but Western India is its chief seat. As already mentioned, the Buddhist excavations in that part of the country are reckoned at 720. Only a very few of the principal can be noticed.

Ajanta.—This village and the ravine celebrated for its cave temples, is situated within the Nizam's Dominions, at the head of one of the *ghâts* leading down from the Ajanta Hills, about 55 miles north-east of Aurangabad. The ravine is wooded, lonely and rugged; the caves are excavated out of a wall of almost perpendicular rock 250 feet high, sweeping round in a semicircle, with the Waghara stream below, and a wooded rocky promontory jutting out from its opposite banks.

Twenty-four *viharas*, or monasteries, and five temples (*chaityas*) have been hewn out of the solid rock, many of them supported by lofty pillars, richly ornamented with sculpture, and covered with paintings.

The cave temples for public worship are usually about twice as long as they are wide, the largest being 94 feet by 41. The back or inner end of the *chaitya* is almost always circular; the roofs are lofty and vaulted. A row of pillars cut out of the solid rock runs round each, dividing the middle from the sides. The columns in the most ancient caves are plain octagonal shafts; in the more modern ones they are richly ornamented. Within the circular end of the cave stands the dagaba (relic-holder) a solid mass of rock, either plain or richly sculptured, consisting of a cylindrical case supporting a cup-shaped *garbha*, which in turn is surmounted by a square capital or tee (*toran.*)

The *viharas* are usually square in form, supported by rows of pillars, either running round them and separating the great central hall from the wings, or disposed in 4 equidistant lines. In the larger caves, a verandah cut out of the rock, and with cells at either end, shades the entrance; the great hall occupies the middle space; with a small chamber behind, and a shrine containing a figure of Buddha enthroned. The walls on all the 3 sides are excavated into cells, the dwelling-places (*grihas*) of the Buddhist monks. The simplest form of the *vihara* is a verandah hewn out of the precipice, with cells opening from the back to the rock.

Few of the caves seem to have been completely finished; but nearly all of them appear to have been painted on the walls, ceilings, and pillars, inside and out. The scenes represented are generally from Buddha's birth stories, the temptation of Mara, hunting scenes, battle-pieces, the carrying off the relics, &c.

Ellora.—The Brahmanical caves have already been described. As already mentioned, 12 of the caves are Buddhist. They differ from those of Ajanta in consequence of their being excavated in the sloping sides of a hill, and not in a nearly perpendicular cliff. From this formation of the ground, almost all the caves at Ellora have court-yards in front of them. Frequently also, an outer wall of rock, with an entrance through it, is left standing; so that the caves are not generally seen from the outside at all.

Karli.—This cave temple, situated on the road between Bombay and Poona, is the largest as well as the most complete Chaitya cave hitherto discovered in India. Inscriptions ascribe its excavation to Maharaja Bhuti, who, according to the Puranas, reigned about 78 B.C.

The temple consists of a central portion and side aisles or wings, terminating in a semicircular vault, round which the aisle is carried. The length inside is 126 feet; the width 45½ feet; the height is about 44 feet. Fifteen pillars on each side separate the nave or centre from the aisles. Each pillar has a tall base, an octagonal shaft, and a richly ornamented capital, on which kneel two elephants, each bearing two figures, generally a man and a woman, but sometimes two females. Immediately under the semicircular dome is the *dagaba*. There are no ornaments on it now; probably it was plastered and painted. It is surmounted by a tee, and on this still stands the remains of an umbrella in wood, very much decayed by age.

The entrance consists of 3 doorways under a gallery. Over the gallery the whole end of the hall is open, forming one great window through which all the light is admitted and thrown upon the dagaba. In front is a screen composed of two stout octagonal pillars, supporting what is now a plain mass of rock. In advance of the screen stands the lion-pillar, supporting 4 lions. A similar pillar probably stood on the other side, but it has either fallen or been taken down to make room for the little temple that now occupies its place. Within a radius of about 20 miles from Karli, there are about 60 caves.

Salsette.—Salsette is an island to the north of Bombay Island, with which it is connected by bridge and causeway. It is noted for its great *Chaitya* cave at Keneri, a copy, though an inferior one, of the Karli cave. It belongs to the beginning of the 5th century, but 9 of its *viharas* seems to be of earlier date. Salsette had, however, a sanctity of its own early in the 4th century as containing a tooth of Buddha. Perhaps from being undisturbed by the troubles of the mainland, the practice of excavating caves lasted longer there than anywhere else. The Buddhist caves faded imperceptibly into those of the Hindu religion, and it is sometimes difficult to draw a line between them.

Stupas and Dagabas.

Sanchi.—Sanchi is a village in the State of Bhopal, Central India, situated on the Betwa river, about 20 miles north-east of Bhopal city. It is famous as the site of some of the most remarkable Buddhist remains in India. They have been described under the name of *the Bhilsa Topes*, as they are only about 5 miles distant from a town of that name.

The present village of Sanchi is situated on a low ridge of sandstone, the general direction of which is from north to south, the whole summit of the hill being covered with ruins. Within a district 10 miles east and west and 6 miles north and south, are 5 or 6 groups of topes, containing altogether between 25 and 30 individual examples. The principal of these is known as the Great Sanchi Tope. There is one great *stupa*, with its railing and other adjuncts; about 10 smaller *stupas*, some now showing nothing more than the foundations; and a stone bowl, 4½ feet in diameter and 2½ feet deep. The village is at present very small, but the numerous ruins scattered over the hill show that there once was a large town on this site.

Nothing is certainly known about the history of these remains. Some suppose that the great stúpa was erected by Asoka, but what it commemorates is unknown.

Two dagabas on the same platform are said to contain relics of Moggalana and Sariputra, friends and companions of Buddha himself, and usually called his right hand and left hand disciples.

Amaravati.—At this place in the Kistna District, north-west of Madras, there were interesting Buddhist remains. The principal have been removed to Madras, where they may be seen in the Museum. The District for some time, both before and after the Christian era, was Buddhist.

BUDDHIST TEMPLES AND REMAINS IN CEYLON.

The opinion of Ceylon or Lanka entertained by most Hindus is gathered from the Ramayana. It is still supposed by many to be inhabited by Rakshasas. The story of the Ramayana is a fable to amuse people. The inhabitants of Lanka say that Rama never came to their island. It is now under the Empress of India.

Ceylon differs from India in containing an account of its history. "The Hindu mind," says the Cambridge Professor of Sanskrit, "seems never to have conceived such an idea as an authentic record of past facts based on evidence. The idlest legend has passed current as the most authentic fact, nay, more readily." On the other hand, the Sinhalese have historical works going back to an early period; the most celebrated of which is called, the *Mahawansa*, or 'Genealogy of the Great.'

The Establishment of Buddhism in Ceylon.

The earliest inhabitants of Ceylon were demon worshippers. It is said that three or four centuries before the Christian era, Wijeyo, descended through his father from the Rajas of Bengal, and through his mother from the royal family of Kalinga, the Telugu country, landed in Ceylon with 700 followers, and made himself king of the Island. Wijeyo and his immediate descendants were Hindus. The eighth sovereign, named Tisso, became celebrated as Devanampiatisso, Tisso the delight of the gods. During his reign Buddhism was first brought to Ceylon.

Tisso being on friendly terms with Asoka,* King of Magadha, sent him a costly present, borne by four Sinhalese noblemen. Asoka received the ambassadors, with great distinction, and sent them back, accompanied by ambassadors of his own, bearing as gifts in return, a crown, a sword of state, water taken from the Ganges, and many other articles. The king, a zealous Buddhist, along with his valuable present, added a recommendation to Tisso to "take refuge in Buddha, his religion, and his priesthood." Asoka likewise sent over his son Mahindo, a Buddhist priest, to aid Tisso in establishing the new religion within his dominions.

Mahindo, who was received by Tisso with great honour, went about preaching, and multitudes became converts. Women came in crowds to hear him, and, headed by the queen Anula, begged to be made priestesses. Mahindo told them that he was unable to comply with their request; but advised them to send for his sister Sanghamitta, a celebrated priestess. An ambassador was accordingly despatched to India to carry the message to Sanghamitta. She immediately informed her father Asoka, but he tried to dissuade her from the undertaking. "Honoured priestess and daughter," said he, "bereft of thee, and separated from my children and grandchildren, what comfort will be left wherewith to lessen my deep sorrow?" But Sanghamitta's devotion to her faith even surpassed her love for her aged parent. She urged the good that might be the result, and the injury which would be caused to their religion by her refusal. The monarch, with a heavy heart, then consented to the departure of his daughter, and she, taking with her a branch of the bo-tree, set sail for Ceylon.

Sanghamitta, on her arrival, prosecuted her object with great zeal and success. The queen and numbers of devoted females, presented themselves, begging to be made priestesses. The bo-tree was planted in a garden, which had been presented by Tisso to Mahindo. With the aid of her brother Mahindo, dagabas* and temples were multiplied, rock temples and cells for priests were scattered over the island, and a cupful of supposed relics was obtained from Asoka. Sanghamitta, satisfied with her labours, spent the remainder of her life in retirement.

* In Sinhalese works he is named *Dharmmasoka*, on account of his merits as a Buddhist.

BO-TREE AT ANURADHAPURA.

Mahindo and his sister devoted their lives to the spread of Buddhism in Ceylon. For this object they gave up princely honours and pleasures, they left their native country, and even their beloved parents and friends. Should not the possessors of the one true religion be willing to make still greater sacrifices on its account?

Tisso erected at Anuradhapura the Thuparámaya dagaba, the most elegant in Ceylon, said to contain the right collar-bone of Buddha. At Mahintalle, a mountain in the neighbourhood, he built thirty-two chambers for priests.

THUPARAMAYA DAGABA.

The 15th Sinhalese King was Dutugemunu. Reflecting upon the innumerable lives sacrificed in his wars, he became anxious about his lot in another world. In the later years of his life, therefore, he devoted all his time and wealth to the erection of viharas and dagabas.

The most extensive work of Dutugemunu was the Lowa Maha Paya, or great Brazen Palace, at Anuradhapura. It was 270 feet square, and the same in height. The apartments rested on 1,600 granite pillars, placed in forty parallel lines, forty pillars in each. The pillars in the middle of the ruin are still nearly twelve feet above the ground. The middle pillars are slightly ornamented, but those on the outer lines are plain, and half their thickness, having been split by wedges. Over these were nine stories, containing 900 apartments, the whole roofed with metal, whence the name.

The interior of the building was magnificent. A spacious hall occupied the centre, adorned with gilt statues of lions and elephants, while at one extremity an ivory throne of beautiful workmanship was erected. The most eminent priests occupied the uppermost stories; those who had fewest claims to sanctity were lodged nearest to the earth. As Sinhalese stairs are very steep, the ascent of nine stories must have been a severe trial to the elder priests, though a breach of the custom by which a superior always occupied a higher seat than his inferiors, would have been tenfold more irksome.

The Ruwanwelle-saya dagaba at Anuradhapura is said to have been 270 feet in height. It is now a round mass of bricks, overgrown with brushwood, and 189 feet high. The base consisted of a square mass of building, 2,000 feet in circumference, paved with large stones of dressed granite, and surrounded by a ditch, seventy feet broad. The sides of the platform were ornamented by the sculptured fore-parts and heads of elephants.

Dutugemunu considering that sacred work should not be done by forced labour, and that the people had suffered much from war, employed hired workmen. The last dagaba, he was unable to finish. To please him, his brother had a frame-work made of wood, covered with cloth, to represent it as complete. Dutugemunu, when very ill, was carried round the dagaba, and laid on a carpet from which it could be seen. Addressing one of his generals, who had become a priest, he said, "In time past, supported by my ten warriors, I engaged in battle; now, single-handed, I commence my last conflict with death, and it is not permitted me to overcome my enemy."

But the dying monarch's command a list was read of his charitable acts. He had constructed 99 viháras, or buildings for priests, at great cost; clothed the whole priesthood three times, giving three garments to each; given two valuable ear ornaments to buy grain during a famine; distributed alms to priests of both sexes from the four quarters without omission; on five different occasions conferred the whole sovereignty of the island on the priesthood for seven days each time; given 7,000 lamps lit with ghee and white wicks in 12 different places; maintained 18 hospitals with doctors and medicines for each; distributed in 44 places rice, sugar, and honey; supplied all the temples in Lanka with lamp-oil for eight days each month; and caused religious discourses to be given in the viháras, endowing the preachers with ghee and cloth. The dying king then said, "All these, done in my days of prosperity, afford no relief to me now; but two offerings which I made in affliction alone give me comfort." After this he expired, gazing on the dagaba, 140 B.C. As he himself said, he had been a slave to the priesthood.

Buddhists in Ceylon imagine themselves to be the most honoured people in the world on account of their supposed possession of the most sacred relic of Buddha, his left canine tooth. Its history may be introduced by some remarks on

Relic Worship.

Adoration of relics constitutes an important point of difference between Hindus and Buddhists. The former are wholly opposed to the practice of preserving the ashes, bones, hair, or teeth of deceased persons, however much such individuals may have been revered during life. In the mind of the Hindus, ideas of impurity are inseparably connected with death, and contamination is supposed to result from contact with the corpses of a man's dearest relatives. Even the living body is regarded as a mass of corruption, a thing to be held in contempt, and a constant impediment to sanctity of life. How much more then ought every part of a dead body to be got rid of without delay! Hence in the present day a corpse is burnt, and its ashes are generally scattered on the surface of sacred rivers or of the sea.

The Buddhist, too, is a thorough Hindu in contemning the living body; but when the corpse of saints has been burnt, he does not scatter the ashes on rivers; he takes pains to preserve them. The calcined ashes, or certain unconsumed portions of the body—such as fragments of bone or hair or nails or teeth—are deposited in relic shrines.

Of course the most sacred of all Buddhist relics are those of Buddha himself. It is said that even before his death portions of his hair and nails were preserved and placed under dagabas. When Buddha's body was burnt, the chief remains, besides the ashes, consisted of four teeth, two cheek bones, and fragments of the skull. Eight princes contended for the

TEMPLE OF THE TOOTH, KANDY, CEYLON.

relics, but in end the matter was settled amicably. Each got a share, and each built a dagaba over his own portion of the relics. The most celebrated of the relics were the four teeth. One of the four is said to have been taken by the gods and another by the Nagas, while the third was taken to Gandhara in the north-west, and the fourth to Kalinga in the south-east.*

THE ORIGINAL TOOTH.

The following account of the Ceylon Dalada, or supposed Tooth Relic, is mainly taken from Tennent's *Ceylon*. Sir J. Emerson Tennent, besides being a man of considerable ability and learning, while holding a high official position in the Island was able to obtain the assistance of the most competent scholars, European and Sinhalese. His work on Ceylon is acknowledged to be one of the best of the kind ever written.

The *Daladawansa*, in Elu or Sinhalese poetry, giving the History of the Tooth, is supposed by Mr. Turnour to have been composed about the year 310 A.D. : there is positive proof, he says, of its being extant at least between A.D. 459 and 477. According to the date commonly accepted by the Sinhalese, Buddha died, 543 B.C. The *Daladawansa* was, therefore, written about 850 years after his death. A Pali translation of this, called the *Dáthá-wansa*, was made in the 12th century by Dhammakitti Thera, during the reign of Queen Lilavati. According to this work, Khema, one of the disciples of Buddha, took the tooth relic from the funeral pile, and gave it to Brahmadatta, king of Kalinga in Dantapura. The king built for it a temple inlaid with gold, where it was worshipped for many generations.

The tooth was afterwards taken to Pataliputra, where it is reported to have worked many miracles. When thrown into a burning furnace, it appeared on the surface of a lotus. An attempt was made to crush it upon an anvil, but it remained embedded in the iron, resisting all the means employed to take it out until Subaddra, a Buddhist, got it removed. Guhasiva, King of Kalinga, afterwards brought back the relic to his own capital, and re-established it in its old temple. When a large army marched against him, before proceeding to the battle-field, he instructed his son-in-law, Dantakumára, who had married his daughter Hemamálá, to carry away the relic to the King of Ceylon in the event of his death. He fell in battle, and his son-in-law and daughter in disguise carried away the relic. They first kept it buried in sand, and after encountering many adventures, Hemamálá hid it in her hair. When they came to the city Tamalitti, they found a ship to take them to Ceylon.

* From *Buddhism*, by Sir Monier Williams.

The Dalada reached Ceylon during the reign of Kirtisri Meghawarna, who is supposed to have ascended the throne in the year 298 A.D., and to have died in 326. The relic was treated with great respect and carefully guarded.

At times the Island suffered greatly from Tamil invasions. Agrabodhi, who began to reign in 769 A.D., unable to expel the Tamils, removed the seat of government from Anuradhapura to Pollonnaruwa, where it remained, with two short interruptions, till 1303 A.D. In that year Bhuwanekabahu I. removed the capital to Yapahu in Seven Korales. The Pandyans took it by surprise, and carried off the Dalada to India. His successor, Prakramabahu IV., went in person to Madura to negotiate its surrender and brought it back to Ceylon.

"During the troublous times which followed," says Tennent, "the original tooth was hidden in different parts of the Island, at Kandy, in Saffragam, and at Kotmalie; but at last in 1560 it was discovered by the Portuguese, taken to Goa by Don Constantine de Braganza, and burnt by the Archbishop in the presence of the Viceroy of India and his court.

"The fate of this renowned relic is so remarkable, and its destruction is related with so much particularity by the Portuguese annalists of the period and their European contemporaries, that no historical doubt can be entertained, even were internal evidence wanting, that the tooth now exhibited at Kandy is a spurious and modern substitute for the original destroyed in 1560."

Sir J. E. Tennent quotes the following account of the destruction of the Dalada from the Portuguese History of Diego de Couto, who was living at the time:

"The King of Burma having heard that the Tooth which was so profoundly revered by all Buddhists, had been carried off, summoned Martino Alfonso, a Portuguese trader then at Pegu with his ship, and besought him on his return to India to entreat the Viceroy to surrender it, offering to give in exchange whatever might be demanded for it. By advice of Martino Alfonso, the king despatched ambassadors to accompany him to the Viceroy on this affair, and empowered them to signify his readiness to ratify any agreement to which they might assent on his behalf.

"Martino Alfonso, on reaching Goa in April 1561, apprised the Viceroy of the arrival of the envoys, who, after their reception, opened their business for which they were accredited, making a request for the tooth in behalf of their sovereign, offering to ratify any terms that might be required, with a proposal for a perpetual alliance with Portugal, and undertaking to provision the fortress of Malacca at all times when called upon, together with many other conditions and promises. The Viceroy promised an early reply; and in the meantime communicated with his veteran captains and fidalgos, all of whom were in favour of accepting an offer which would recruit the exhausted treasury; and so eager were they, that the question seemed to be decided.

"But the matter having reached the ear of the Archbishop Don Gaspar, he repaired instantly to the Viceroy, and warned him that he was not to permit the tooth to be ransomed for all the treasure in the universe; since it would be dishonouring to the Lord and afford an opportunity to those idolaters to pay to that bone the worship which belonged to God alone. The Archbishop wrote memorials on the subject, and preached against it from the pulpit in the presence of the Viceroy and his court, so that Don Constantine, who as a conscientious Catholic feared God and obeyed the Church, hesitated to proceed with the affair and to take any step that was not unanimously approved. He therefore convened an assembly of the Archbishop, the prelates and heads of the religious orders, together with the captains and senior fidalgos and other officers of his Government. He laid the matter before them, the large offers of money that had been made for the tooth and the pressing wants of the service, all of which could be provided for out of so great a ransom. After mature deliberation a resolution was come to that it was not competent to part with the tooth, since its surrender would be an incitement to idolatry, and an insult to the Almighty—events which could not be contemplated, though the State or even the world itself might be imperilled. Of this opinion were the prelates, the inquisitors, the vicar-general of the Dominicans, the prior of Goa, the father custodian of the Franciscans and others.

"This resolution having been come to and committed to writing to which all attached their signatures (and a copy of which is now in our possession in the Record Office), the Viceroy called on the Treasurer to produce the tooth. He handed it to the Archbishop, who in their presence placed it in a mortar and with his own hand reducing it to powder, cast the pieces into a brazier, which stood ready for the purpose; after which the ashes and the charcoal together were cast into the river in sight of all, they crowding to the verandah and windows which looked upon the water.

"Many protested against this measure of the Viceroy, since there was nothing to prevent the Buddhists from making other idols; and out of a piece of bone they could shape another tooth in resemblance of the one they had lost, and extend to it the same worship; whilst the gold that had been rejected would have repaired the pressing necessities of the State.

"To commemorate the event and illustrate the spirit which had dictated an act approved by the Fathers of the Company and signalised by zeal for Christianity and the glory of God, a device was designed as follows: On an escutcheon was a representation of the Viceroy and the Archbishop surrounded by the prelates, monks, and divines, who had been present on the occasion, and in the midst was a burning brazier, together with Buddhists offering purses of money. Above the letter C, being the initial of Don Constantine, was repeated five times, thus,

C C C C C

and below it the five words

Constantinus cœli cupidine crumenas cremavit.

The interpretation being that, "Constantine, devoted to heaven, rejected the treasures of earth."*

The Second Tooth.

The way in which the second Tooth was manufactured, is thus described by Sir J. E. Tennent:

"The King of Pegu, in 1566, having been told that he was to wed a Sinhalese princess, sent to demand her in marriage; but the reigning sovereign, Don Juan Dharmapala, having unfortunately no child, the prophecy was on the point of discomfiture, when his chamberlain, a nobleman of the blood royal, suggested the substitution of his own daughter, and added impiety to fraud by feigning to the Peguan envoys that he still held in secret the genuine relic, falsely supposed to have been destroyed by the Christians at Goa. The device was successful and the supposititious princess was received in Pegu with all the nuptial honours of royalty; and ambassadors were despatched to Ceylon to obtain possession of the sacred tooth which was forthwith transferred to Arracan."

Tennent gives full details from the history of de Couto, who lived at the time. When the supposed tooth reached Burma, the priesthood assembled, the people crowded devoutly to offer adoration to it, and it was placed in a splendid temple.

The Third Tooth.

Tennent says: "The king of Kandy, Wikrama Bahu, on learning the deception which had been perpetrated by his cousin of Cotta, apprised the Pegu sovereign of the imposture which had been practised upon him: and to redress it he offered his own daughter in marriage, and proposed to send as her dowry the veritable tooth, affirming that both the one recently obtained from Colombo and the other formerly pulverised at Goa were counterfeit, his alone being the genuine relic of Buddha. But the Prince of Pegu was too devout to confess himself a dupe."

"The incidents of de Couto's narrative are too minute, and their credibility is established by too many contemporaneous and even current authorities to admit of any doubt that the authenticity of the tooth now preserved in the Maligawa at Kandy is no higher than its antiquity, and that the supposed relic is a clumsy substitute manufactured by Wikrama Bahu in 1566 to replace the original relic destroyed by the Portuguese in 1560. The dimensions and form of the present relic are fatal to any belief of its identity, with the one originally worshipped, which was probably human, whereas the object now shown is a piece of discoloured ivory about 2 inches in length, and less than one in diameter, resembling the tooth of a crocodile rather than that of a man."

* Tennent's *Ceylon*, Vol. II., pp. 213-215.

"The popular acceptance, notwithstanding this anomalous shape, may probably be accounted for by the familiarity of the Kandyans under their late kings, with the forms of some of the Hindu divinities, occasionally depicted with similarly projecting canines."

Tennent says, "The Sinhalese never seem to have been scrupulous about multiplying Buddha's teeth." Kublai Khan was a very powerful emperor of China. He demanded tribute from the king of Pegu. As his ambassadors were insolent, the king of Pegu, against the advice of his ministers, put them to death. Kublai Khan then invaded Burma and plundered the capital. About the year 1281, he demanded and obtained from the king of Ceylon two large back teeth, together with some of Buddha's hair, in a handsome stone vessel. This is recorded by Marco Polo, a famous Venetian traveller, who was for several years in the service of Kublai Khan.

THE SUPPOSED TOOTH.

Exhibition of the Tooth.

The relic is kept in what is called the *Dalada Maligawa* at Kandy, the old capital, in the centre of the Island. The building is not very large, and was situated within the enclosure of the old palace of the kings. In front there is an ornamental stone wall.

The tooth is suspended by a piece of gold wire over a golden lotus, as shown in the above picture. It is covered with bell-shaped shrines, for which there are three keys, kept by the temple chief and two priests. It is contained within a small room without windows, and only a door in front. When a priest draws back the curtain, the worshippers can look inside to the shrine.

The tooth itself is very seldom exhibited. The last exhibition during a Sinhalese king was in the reign of Kirti Sri, about 1775. In 1828 there was a grand exhibition, as represented in the picture. Of late years it has sometimes been shown privately to distinguished visitors. Thus the Prince of Wales saw it when he visited Kandy in 1876.

A few years ago money was wanted for the repair of the temple. To raise it, there was an exhibition of the Dalada, when pilgrims swarmed from all parts of the Sinhalese provinces to gaze on the precious relic, and pour their offerings into its treasury.

An English lady, Miss Gordon Cumming, skilful in painting, was then in Kandy. She saw the relic day after day, and made the very correct drawing of it, shown in the picture.

WORSHIP OF THE TOOTH.

The supposed tooth is about two inches long, and about the thickness of a lady's forefinger. It is only a piece of discoloured ivory, manufactured by Wikrama Bahu, and never was the tooth of a human being. As already described, the real tooth was destroyed at Goa.

THE PERAHARA, OR PROCESSION.

The Perahara.

The kings of Ceylon were chiefly of Tamil descent, and originally Hindus. In [illegible]dy there are several Hindu temples. It was customary to have an annual procession in honor of the Hindu gods, called the Perahara, without any reference to Buddhism. In 1775 the king of Ceylon had invited some Siamese priests to come to the island to restore the highest order of Buddhist priesthood. These hearing the noisy preparations for the festival, and learning that it was solely in honour of Hindu gods, made a complaint to the king. That evening he ordered that the shrine should be carried at the head of the procession in his own howdah, and that thus the ceremony should be in honour of Buddha as well as the gods. The priests take no part in the procession beyond lending the temple elephants and the shrine supposed to contain the tooth, together with a silver gilt canopy. The tooth itself is not taken out.

The procession takes place at night amid the glare of torches, the beating of tom-toms, the clanging of brass cymbals, the shriek of shrill pipes, the blowings of conch shells, and contortions of masked devil-dancers. The elephant bearing the shrine has gorgeous trappings, with an image of Buddha enthroned embroidered on the cloth covering its forehead. Its tusks are also decorated.

Sripada, the Sacred Foot-print.

Next in importance to the worship of relics by the Buddhists, is that of foot-prints. The worshippers of Vishnu will not leave their houses in the morning without marking their foreheads with the symbol of Vishnu's feet. The Buddhists do not imitate this practice, but they make long and toilsome pilgrimages to bow down before what they believe to be the impression of Buddha's foot on a rock.

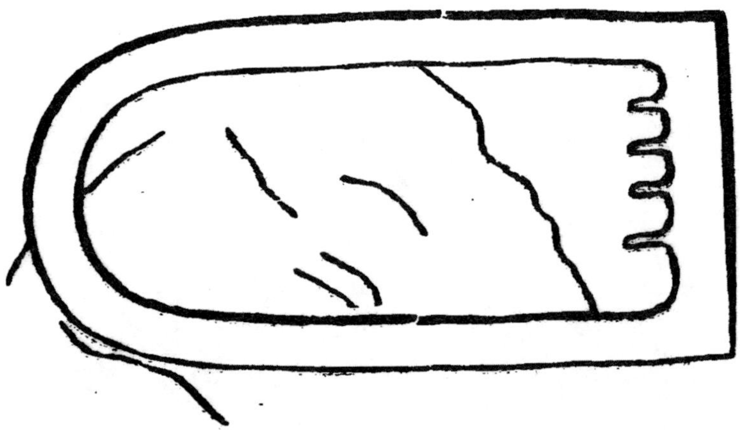

SUPPOSED FOOT-PRINT.

On the top of Adam's Peak, a high mountain in Ceylon, there is what is called *Sripada*, a supposed foot-print of Buddha. The writer of this account spent hours on the Peak, and was able carefully to examine the alleged foot-print. The picture above was drawn on the spot. There is only a little hollow in the rock, some parts of which are deeper than others, represented in the picture by dark lines. The likeness to the foot is made entirely with chunam or lime. Even if it were like a foot-print, this would not prove it to be real. Any mason can, in a short time, cut out one.

The story is that Buddha left the print of one foot on Adam's Peak, and then, in one stride, strode across to Siam, where he left the impression of his other foot.

The Siamese hold their foot-print in as much reverence as the Sinhalese hold theirs. Its appearance is like that of the foot-print on Adam's Peak. Nothing is to be seen but a hollow in the rock. Likeness to a foot there is none.

The supposed Height of Buddha.

Buddhists generally believe that Buddha was very much taller than an ordinary man. Eighteen cubits is a common reckoning; an image in Japan is 32 cubits. A reclining image at Cotta is said to be 28 cubits long.

The Sripada at Adam's Peak is about 5 feet 8 inches long. A well-proportioned man is about six times the height of the length of his foot. At the above rate, tested by the Sripada, Buddha was 34 feet in height.

A little consideration will show the absurdity of this. How could a giant 34 feet high have a wife of about 6 feet? How could people have reached up to his bowl to give him alms? How could he have entered ordinary houses? The people would have fled in terror from such a monster.

As already mentioned, the Jains profess to have 24 saints, like Buddhas. The first they say, was 500 poles in height, about 1½ miles, and lived for 8,400,000 years! The second was 450 poles in height, and his age declined to 7,200,000 years. The downward movement continued until the last two were human in regard to size and length of life. Wisdom is not to be measured by magnitude. The little ant is wiser than some huge animals.

GIGANTIC JAPANESE IMAGE OF BUDDHA.

Unless Buddha was about 34 feet in height, he could not have had a foot 5 feet 8 inches long. The absurdity of supposing him to have been of that height has been shown. What is the inference? That the pretended foot-print, like the pretended tooth, is an imposture. It is a mere hollow in the rock, without any resemblance to a foot. Simple-minded people have been deceived into the belief that they may make pilgrimages to it, and present offerings.

BUDDHIST BUILDINGS IN BURMA.

COUNTRY.

BURMA is a large country, now forming the eastern portion of the Indian Empire. It formerly included Assam, Hill Tipperah, and Manipur. At present the two chief divisions are *Lower* and *Upper Burma*. The former has an area of 87,000 square miles—rather less than that of the Central Provinces—with a population in 1891 of 5 millions. Upper Burma contains about 190,000 square miles—nearly as large as Bengal and Assam taken together,—but the population is only about 3 millions. The entire area is nearly 280,000 square miles,—larger than the Madras and Bombay Presidencies united, with a population of only about 8 millions.

Some parts of India are sandy deserts, where rain seldom falls. Burma, on the contrary, from its abundant supply of rain, especially on the coast, is covered with luxuriant vegetation.

The country gradually slopes from the wild and mountainous region in the north to the delta of the Irawadi. It is intersected by mountain ranges, running north and south, between which flow the principal rivers the *Irawadi*, the *Sittaung*, and the *Salwin*.

Vegetable Productions.—Rice (of which the Burmese count 102 different sorts) is the chief crop. The level country forms one vast rice-field. It is by far the most important export, and the prosperity of Lower Burma is mainly due to it. The value of the rice exported is about 6 crores of rupees. Teak timber is next in importance. The trees are felled in the forests, the logs are dragged by elephants to rivers, and floated down during the rains. Tobacco is largely grown, but as all the Burmese are inveterate smokers, a considerable quantity has to be imported from India. Sugar is obtained chiefly from the palmyra palm ;

sugar-cane is little cultivated. The plantain is the staple fruit; but mangoes, the guava, the orange, and others, are also common. The durian, a fruit with a very strong smell, is grown in the south. The bamboo is plentiful, and largely used for houses and many other purposes.

People.—Burma is inhabited by several races. The Burmese proper are short, stout, well-made, of a brown complexion, with coarse abundant black hair on the head, and rarely any on the face. They are considered intermediate between the Chinese and Malays. The Burmese excel in wrestling, rowing, football, and other athletic exercises; they are clever as carpenters and smiths.

The name the Burmese give their own race is Mran-ma (as written), corrupted commonly into Ba-má, and from this the various forms of Burma appear to have been taken.

There are several races scattered over the country.

Talaings.—The aborigines of Lower Burma are supposed to have been the Muns. Indians from Telingana, south of Orissa, several centuries before the Christian era, came for purposes of trade to the tract about the mouths of the Irawadi, Sittaung, and Salwin, then called Suvarana Bhúmí. They intermarried with the Muns, and their descendants received the title of Talaings from the name of the country whence the colonists had sailed. This name was extended in later times to all Muns.

The Talaings differ little in appearance from the Burmese. Their features are perhaps more regular, the nose is not so flat, and the face is longer.

Karens.—Next to the Burmese, the Karens are the most numerous race in Lower Burma. Their tradition is that they came from Central Asia, across the great Desert of Gobi, the "Sea of Rolling Sand," about 13 centuries ago. A number of them have become Christians.

The *Chins* are a wild tribe in Upper Burma. They tattoo the faces of their young girls to such an extent as not to leave even an eyelid untouched.

Disposition.—The Burmese is calm and contented. He does not want to grow rich. When he does make a large sum of money, he spends it all on some pious work or on a feast. He jogs on through a cheerful existence, troubled by no anxious cares and free from all temptations of ambition. His daily round is simple enough. In the morning after his bath, he loiters about, talking to the neighbours till breakfast time, or perhaps strolls out to the corner of his paddy-field, and indulges in a smoke. After breakfast he probably dozes through the heat of the day, and when the shadows begin to get long, saunters about again. A semblance of regular labour appears when the paddy is being sown or the grain reaped, but even then no one is in the least inclined to disturb himself for the sake of rapid work. The evenings are spent ordinarily at a play during the fine season, or in converse over a cheroot at a friend's house during the rains. Variety comes occasionally in the shape of a hilarious journey to a distant pagoda feast, or a trip down the river. His greatest ambition is to see the village boat successful at the races, and the village champion cock or buffalo triumphant over all competitors.

A BURMESE OFFICER.

The Women.—A Burmese does not work for his living if he can help it. He seems to believe that his womankind were sent into the world to save him trouble. The women share this belief, and do their allotted work like men.

Women in Burma occupy a much freer and happier position than they do in Indian social life. They go about freely; manage the household, buy the daily supplies in the bazaar, and in every respect take an active part in domestic affairs.

There is hardly a single house in a whole village where something is not offered for sale; a few dried fish, betel nuts, cardamoms, cocoa-nuts, cheap knives, &c. Where there are many girls about the house, cloths are woven at odd times in the loom which stands in the compound or in a corner of the verandah of every house.

A BURMESE WOMAN WASHING HER HAIR.

The Burmese wives make successful women of business. They conduct not merely retail trades, but also large wholesale concerns on account of their husbands, and are very good hands at driving a bargain.

Like their sex in some other countries, Burmese women, when angry, use the most abominable language.

Food.—The staple article is plain boiled rice, which is piled up in a heap on a huge platter, round which the household arrange themselves, sitting on their heels. The curry which is taken with it is placed in little bowls, and each one of the party has his own plate, and helps himself. Spoons and forks and Chinese chopsticks are unknown. Ordinarily the curry consists of a soup, in which chillies and onion figure largely. The other ingredients are very various. Tamarind leaves and those of the mango-tree are used by the very poor. Along with the curry, which has always much salt and oil in it, there are a variety of condiments, especially the strongly flavoured fish-paste, without which no Burmese would consider his meal complete.

After meals every one smokes—men, women, and children. The ordinary Burmese cheroot is very mild. The cigar for home consumption, known as the green cheroot, is very large, from 6 to 8 inches long, and about an inch in diameter, at one end and tapering to half that breadth at the other. In the manufacture of it, chopped tobacco leaves and pieces of the stem of the tobacco plant and the pith of a species of Euphorbia, are the chief ingredients. The cover is often made of the leaf of the teak-tree; a piece of red raw silk fastens it at the end put in the mouth. All Burmese ladies are clever at rolling cheroots.

Chewing betel is carried on in the interval between smokes.

Dress.—Both sexes are proud of the length of their hair, and it is not uncommon to see it reaching below the knee and down to the ankles. The men wear it in a knot on the top of the head; the women gather it behind. Both men and women are in the habit of adding to its size by interweaving false tresses.

The full dress of a rich man is simple and picturesque. A silk cloth, 15 cubits long and about 2½ wide, is wound round, covered with a short white cotton jacket, over which a dark or coloured cloth one is often worn. Round the head a flowered silk handkerchief is loosely worn as a turban. Poor people have only strips of cotton cloth; but nearly every person has some article of silk.

Women wear a simple piece of cotton or silk, almost square, 4½ feet long by about 5 broad, and woven in two pieces of different patterns. This is wound tightly over the bosom, and fastened with a simple twist of the ends. A loose cotton jacket is also worn, and over the shoulders is thrown a bright silk handkerchief, the same as that used by the men for turbans. Nothing is worn on the head except flowers, twisted into the hair.

Valuable gold ornaments are reserved for special occasions.

Houses.—Although the pagodas and temples of Burma are remarkable for grandeur, most of the Burmese live in flimsy bamboo huts, and even rich men seldom think of building for themselves fine houses. The cause of this is probably found in the regulations of the Burmese Government. Brick houses were forbidden; gilding was not allowed, and permission to paint the pillars of a house was granted to very few. All houses are one-storied, for it would be a degradation to have the feet of some one over your head.

A Burmese house stands on posts, so that the floor is seven or eight feet from the

BURMESE VILLAGE.

ground. This protects it from damp, and from inundation during the rains. The house often consists of only one room, usually however of two or more, and to the front of the house there is always a verandah, three or four feet lower than the house.

The posts which form the main portion of the house are usually six in number, and all have their names. An astrologer must decide whether a place is lucky to build on, and when it should be commenced. Posts are masculine, feminine, and neuter. Male posts are of equal size at both ends; females are larger at the bottom; those which swell out at the middle are neuter. Luck, good or bad, is supposed to depend upon the choice of the posts.

Poor people use bamboo instead of wood, and make their walls of mats, woven of the same substance split up.

School and entering a Monastery.—Buddhism is the religion of the Burmese. The priests or monks are called *pungyis*, meaning "great glory," and the monasteries in which they live are called *kyoungs*. It was formerly the custom for every boy in Burma, when he reached the age of about 8 years, to go to a kyoung. Every Buddhist boy was taught to read and write; but it was not thought necessary to teach girls.

About one in four of the population of Burma is able to read or is under instruction, while in India the proportion is only about one in twenty.

Until a Buddhist has assumed, at least for a time, the yellow robes of a monk, he cannot claim to be more than a mere animal. It is not till he has subjected himself to the discipline of the kyoung, that he can reap the fruits of good actions in former births, and can look forward to a more glorious future. The novice drops his secular name, and receives a new honorific name, to mark that it is now open to him to escape from suffering. He loses the name when he returns to the world again, but it is sufficient that he has once borne it.

A candidate must have reached the age of 20 years, and have obtained his parents' permission. His friends provide him with the eight articles which a monk cannot do without. These are three pieces of yellow cloth for dress, a begging bowl, suspended from the neck, a leathern girdle, a razor to shave his head and beard, a needle to stitch his clothes, and a water-strainer to prevent the destruction of animal life.

Although every male should thus become a monk, there is no fixed time for wearing the yellow robes. In a few cases, the novice comes back again the same night, and assumes the lay dress. Others remain only 24 hours, long enough to enable them to go once at least round the village begging from door to door. But it is not considered decent to leave under a week. Some stay longer—a fortnight, a month or two months. The more earnest remain at least one *Wah* or *Was*, the months of the rainy season. A fervent Buddhist remains three Wahs, one for his father, one for his mother, and one for himself.

The novice in the monastery must go on with his studies. He has also to attend the monks, laying before them their daily food, water, the betel box, and whatever else they require. Every morning he must go round with the begging bowl strapped round his neck. He should eat only the food thus presented, but rich parents sometimes send meals daily, or even employ a cook to prepare his food.

Strict discipline is maintained. The novices are not allowed to go out at night. Breaches of this rule are severely punished. The culprit's hands are tied high above his head, and his naked back is beaten with a stout bamboo.

Buddhist Monks in Burma.

There are five Buddhist commands considered binding on all: 1. Not to take life. 2. Not to steal. 3. Not to commit adultery. 4. Not to tell lies. 5. Not to drink intoxicating liquors. Some take upon themselves three additional commands: 6. Not to eat after noon. 7. Not to attend dancing, stage plays, &c. 8. Not to use perfumes. Monks are bound to observe two more: 9. Not to use high beds or couches. 10. Not to receive gold or silver. This last command is often violated. Some monks receive money—covered with a handkerchief. Others will tell their pupils to take the coin and put it in a box.

BUDDHIST MONKS RETURNING WITH FOOD COLLECTED.

In the early morning in all the towns and villages of Burma are to be seen rows of monks, walking slowly along the streets, with their alms-bowl slung round their necks, into which the people pour food as they pass. They are barefooted, and have no covering for the head. In the right hand they carry a large palm-leaf fan, which they hold before their face in the presence of women, so that no evil thought may enter the mind. They are forbidden to ask for food, to look to the right or to the left; and they may not enter or loiter about the doors of houses. Gautama said: "The wise priest never asks for anything; it is a proper object for which he carries the alms-bowl; and this is his only mode of solicitation." When anything is poured into their bowls, they do not return thanks, but content themselves by saying, "Well, well." When sufficient has been obtained to appease their hunger, they return to the monasteries to eat it.

Many Burmese consider it a great act of merit to make a vow never to partake of a meal without reserving a portion of it for the monks. Nothing whatever should be cooked in monasteries. The hours during which food can be eaten are only between sunrise and noon.

The duties of the monks are not heavy. They generally lead a lazy life. Occasionally they read the sacred books on a feast day or go to a funeral that the pious may have an opportunity of giving them presents, and to lay up a good store of merit for future births. It is chiefly as teachers of the young that they deserve the support of the people.

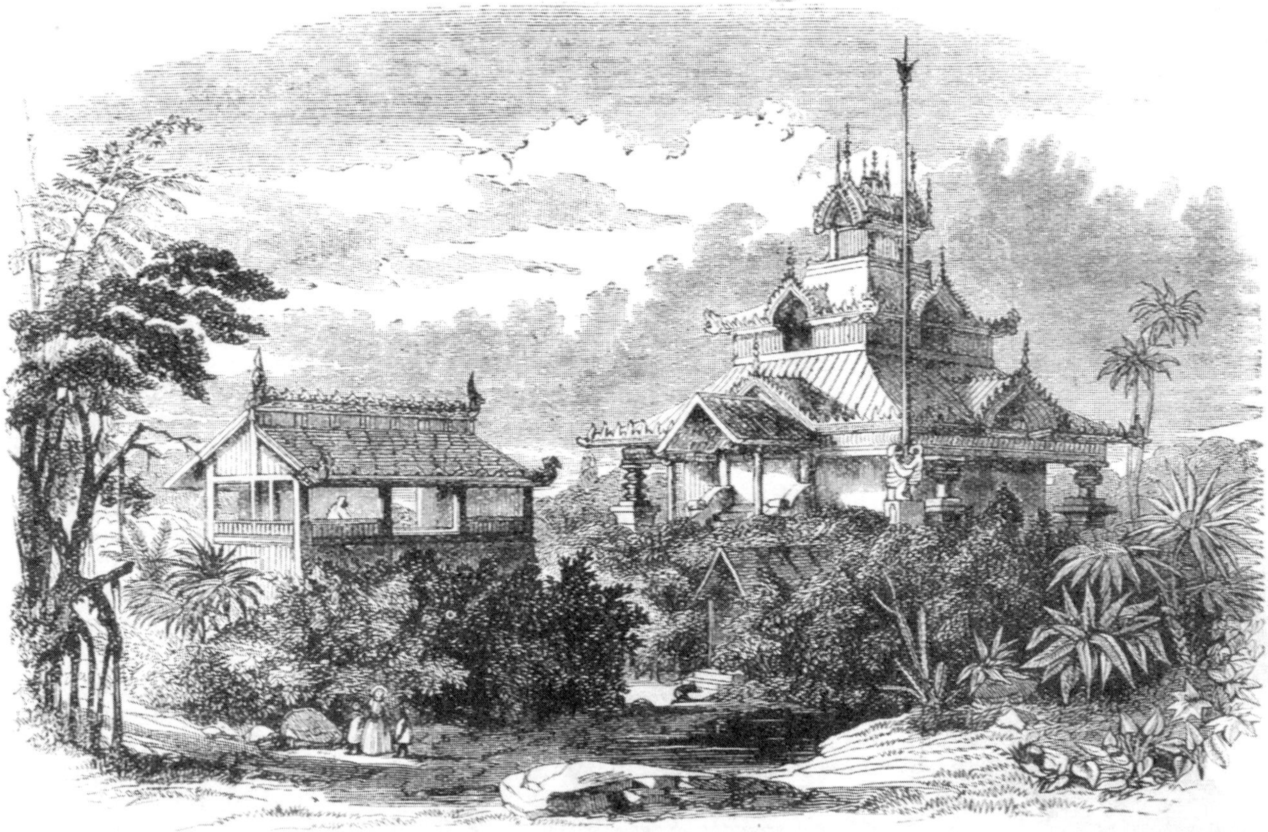

BUDDHIST BUILDINGS.

These are of three principal kinds :

Kyoungs.—As already mentioned, these are the monasteries in which the monks live. Ordinarily they are built of teak, though in many places brick buildings are being erected, notwithstanding the prejudice that exist against them from their greater liability to damage in the case of earthquakes. The shape is always oblong, and the inhabited portion of wooden buildings is raised on posts or pillars 8 or 10 feet above the ground. They are, like all the other houses in the country, never more than one storey high, for it is an indignity to have any one over a person's head—especially in the case of a monk. The space between the ground and the floor is never used except by school boys and a few pariah dogs. A flight of steps of stone or wood leads up to the verandah.

The building has tier upon tier of massive roofs, giving the appearance of many storeys when there is actually but one. This style of roofing was allowed only for religious buildings, for the royal palaces, and for the houses as a special favour of a few high officials. The ends of the gables are adorned with pinnacles, each with a curious wooden flag at the top, and crowned with an umbrella, called a *htee*, gilt and furnished with bells, the whole being elaborately carved.

The area of the large compound in which the monastery stands is enclosed by a high fence. All within is sacred ground, and even a prince, when he arrives on an elephant, must dismount at the gate, and come in reverently barefooted.

The majority of kyoungs are plain teak wood or brick and lime structures, with more or less carving and decorations. The gorgeous buildings of this kind are at Mandalay. The Royal Monastery is the most striking collection of edifices of their kind to be seen in the world. Every building is magnificent ; the whole ablaze with gold leaf and fragments of looking glass, embedded in a resinous gum, while the zinc roofs glisten like silver in the sun, and the bells on the gable spires tinkle melodiously to every breeze. The huge posts are gilt all over or covered with red lacqueredware ; eaves and gables represent all kinds of fantastic and grotesque figures.

SACRED POSTS.

Pagodas.—As already explained, this word is more correctly *dagaba*, derived from the Sanskrit *dhatu garba*, a relic shrine. It is properly applied only to monuments raised over some of the supposed remains of Buddha or articles belonging to him. The word pagoda is not known to the Burmese. Such a building is called a *Zaydee*.

Zaydees are of many shapes. The monks say that Buddha left no instructions regarding them, except that a small mound should be raised over his bones in the form of a heap of rice. The relics are placed in the centre. Miniature pagodas and monasteries in silver and gold, precious stones, &c., are also enclosed. A gold image of Buddha, with the hooded snake raising itself over him, is never wanting.

In Lower Burma the pagodas are all solid pyramidal cones, rising with a gradual diminishing rounded outline, and surmounted by a htee or umbrella spire, formed of concentric rings, lessening to a rod with a small vane at the top. They are almost without exception erected on more or less elevated platforms.

Temples.—These are erected to contain images of Buddha and for worship. They are generally made of wood richly carved. Images of Buddha represent him in three principal attitudes,—standing, sitting cross-legged, and reclining. As already mentioned, they are made of white marble, in large numbers, to the north of Mandalay.

Sir Monier Williams says: "It was indeed by a strange irony of fate that the man who denied any god or any being higher than himself, and told his followers to look to themselves alone for salvation, should have been not only deified and worshipped, but represented by more images than any other being ever idolized in any part of the world . . . . Not only are isolated images manufactured out of all kinds of materials, but rows on rows are sculptured in relief, and the greater the number the greater religious merit."

The worshippers, if men, sit on their heels. The body is bent forward, and the hands are joined together and raised to the forehead. The women kneel down together, and take special care to cover their feet. All are barefooted. Before commencing the repetition of

BURMESE TEMPLE.

the formulæ, three prostrations are made with the forehead to the ground, and the same is repeated at the close. On rising to depart, the worshipper turns to the right. It is usual to hold some offering between the hands during the ceremony—a prayer-flag, a flower, or something of the kind—and this is afterwards reverently deposited on the altar.

The Buddhists do not pray in the strict sense of the word: Buddha is supposed to have entered nirwana, and no longer exists. Many only repeat the formula:

I make Buddha my refuge,
I make his Law my refuge;
I make his Assembly my refuge.

To this is often added, "Change, pain, illusion," repeated on the rosary.

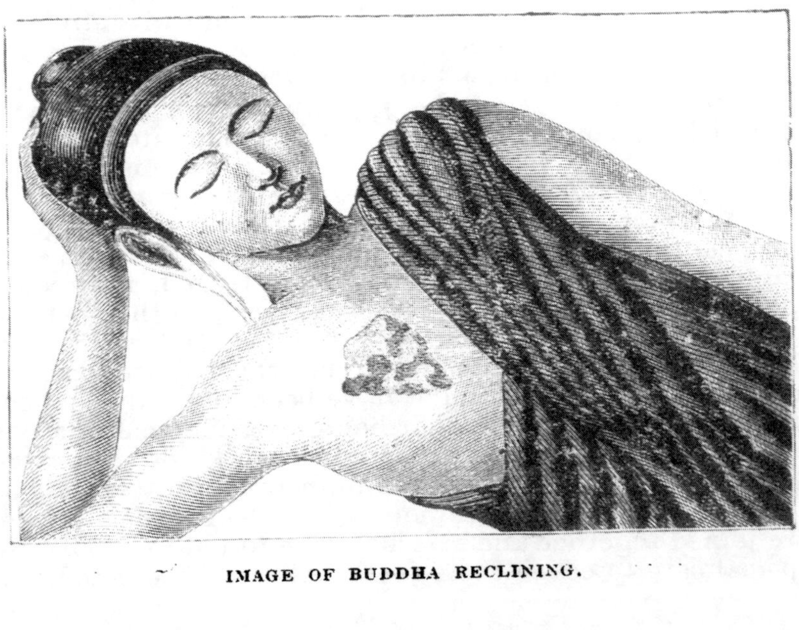

IMAGE OF BUDDHA RECLINING.

BURMESE VIEW.

It is a work of merit to go about lighting tapers and candles which have been blown out or lamps which have got choked up, watering flowers, and so on.

The prayer-flags are made of paper, cut fancifully into figures of dragons, lizards, and the like, with embroidery work round the edges. In the centre is written some pious reflection or aspiration, and the offerer places it on the shrine. The following are samples of inscriptions:

"By means of this paper the offerer will become very strong."
"By the merit of this paper Wednesday's children will be blessed by spirits and men."
"May the man born on Friday gain reward for his pious offering."
"May the man born on Monday be freed from sickness and from the Three Calamities."

Bells.—The Burmese are remarkable for their love of bells. Every large pagoda has some dozens of them of all sizes. One or two were put up with the central shrine itself; others have been added at various times as offerings.

The bells are not intended, as in Christian countries, to summon worshippers to their devotions. Their use is to direct attention to the fact of the praise of Buddha having been recited. The worshipper, when he has finished, goes to one of the bells and strikes it three times, to bring to the notice of the guardian spirits and the four worlds what he has been doing. There are always a number of deers' antlers and billets of wood lying near the bell for this purpose.

The Burmese bells are not handsome in shape. They come straight down to the mouth like a barrel, not expanding at the rim, but their tone is sweet. Some of them are very large.

A few of the principal Pagodas will now be described :—

RANGOON.

RANGOON, the capital of Lower Burma, is situated on the east bank of a branch of the Irawadi, 21 miles from the sea.

The tradition is that the first village on the site of modern Rangoon was founded about 585 B.C., by two brothers, who are said to have passed with 500 carts of merchandise

IMAGES, SUPPOSED TO REPRESENT LIONS, AT THE ENTRANCE OF A PAGODA, AT PROME.

through a forest in which Gautama was then residing. They made an offering of honey to Gautama, and entreated that he would bestow upon them something that they might honour as a relic. He therefore gave them 8 hairs of his head, which they brought to their own country. These were enshrined in a pagoda, since known as the Shway (golden) Dagon, near the modern town of Rangoon.

Alompra, after overcoming the Peguans, came down to Dagon, and repaired the great pagoda. He also, for the most part, rebuilt the town, and gave it the name of Ran-Kun (the end of the war) which it has ever since borne. Rangoon, however, remained little more than a group of hovels, just above the level of high tide.

About 1790, the English obtained leave to establish a factory in Rangoon, and it gradually improved. In 1852 it came into their possession. Within six months, steps were taken for laying out regular streets, for raising the general level, and for keeping out the river.

The pagoda stands on a small hill, which has been graduated into successive terraces, sustained by brick walls. The summit is completely levelled. The pagoda rises to the height of 370 feet. It is surrounded by monasteries, uncouth colossal lions, posts with flags, and a multitude of idols. In the morning, men and women are seen in every direction, kneeling behind their gifts and reciting their devotions; aged persons sweep out every place, and pick the grass from the crevices as a work of merit; the large bells send forth frequent sounds. Every one brings a present, often a bunch of flowers, but generally the nicest food already cooked. Great stone vessels stand round the pagoda, into which the worshippers lay their leafy plates of rice, plantains, cakes, &c. As these are filled, the pagoda servants empty them into their vessels. Dogs and crows struggle around the altars, devouring the recent offerings. Pilgrims come to this pagoda, even from Siam, China, and Corea.

Prome.

Prome is situated on the Irawadi, about 160 miles north of Rangoon. At one time it was the capital of a powerful kingdom. The population is now about 30,000. Shwe-san-daw, the principal pagoda, is situated on a hill about half a mile from the Irawadi, and rises from a nearly square platform to the height of 80 feet. It is surrounded by 83 small golden temples, each containing an image of Buddha. Many marvels are told of the erection of this pagoda. It is said to have been raised on an emerald box, resting on 7 ingots of gold, in which were deposited 3 hairs of Buddha himself. Successive kings and governors have added to and embellished the building. The annual festival in March is attended by thousands of devout Buddhists. The Shwe-nat-daw Pagoda, about 16 miles south of Prome, also stands on high ground. Immediately below it is a plain, where, early in the year, as many as 20,000 pilgrims sometimes assemble for the annual 8 days' festival held here. The Burmese chronicles relate that the pagoda was originally built by the wife of Dut-ta-baung, who reigned from 443 to 372 B.C. This king granted to the pagoda and set apart for its use for ever, the whole space of ground around it on which its shadow fell between sunrise and sunset.

Pagan.

Pagan is situated on the Irawadi about 160 miles north of Prome and about 70 miles below Amarapura, the former capital of Burma. There were two cities, called Old and New Pagan. The empire of Prome came to an end, it is said, through civil strife, and one of the princes in A.D. 107, flying to the north, established himself at Pagan, where the Burmese monarchy continued under a succession of about 50 princes to the end of the 13th century. This refers to Old Pagan. Its site is now a complete jungle, but covered with the remains of brick buildings as far as the eye can reach. There are also the ruins of several large dagabas, which have now more the appearance of earthen mounds than the remains of brick buildings, and they are covered with jungle to the top.

In the 13th century, Kublai Khan, the Mongol emperor of China, demanded tribute from Burma. The Mongol ambassadors were insolent, and the Burmese King, against the remonstrance of his ministers, put them to death. The Mongols invaded Burma. The Burmese were defeated in a great battle; the king fled from Pagan, which the Mongols entered and plundered about 1284 A.D. The city, though deserted, still contains the remains

BUDDHIST BUILDINGS AT PAGAN.

of about a hundred buildings, some of them stupendous, and in a wonderful state of preservation after six centuries.

Pagan, besides pagodas, contains numerous temples, with large halls devoted to images and image worship. Some are in good preservation, with superb carved and gilded ceilings. Others are in ruins.

MANDALAY.

MANDALAY, the capital of Upper Burma, is about two miles east of the Irawadi, on a level plain at the foot of an isolated hill. The father of Theebaw transferred the seat of Government to Mandalay from the neighbouring city of AMARAPURA in 1860. AVA also adjoining, founded in 1364, was the usual capital until the foundation of Amarapura in 1783, and was again the capital for a time.

THE INCOMPARABLE PAGODA, MANDALAY.

The city is laid out in a square, each side of which is a little over a mile in length. It is enclosed by a brick wall, 26 feet high, and 3 feet thick. The wall is pierced with 12 gates, 3 on each side. A deep moat, 100 feet broad, extends along the four sides, and is always kept full of water. It is crossed by 5 bridges.

The palace occupies the central space in the city. The outermost enclosure consists of a stockade of teakwood posts, 20 feet high, and within it are three successive enclosures, bounded by brick walls. The front of the palace, which faces the east, contains the Great Hall of Audience, 260 feet long, composed of teak timber, elaborately carved and gilded, erected on a terrace of brick-work, 10 feet high. Behind this hall are the Privy Council Chamber and other offices; and to the westward are the private apartments and the pleasure-grounds.

The most celebrated pagoda in Burma is the great "Arakan Pagoda" of Mandalay. It contains a brass image of Buddha, represented sitting, which it is said was brought over from Akyab, in the year 1784 A.D. The shrine in which it stands is one of the most splendid in the country. The image itself is covered with a great seven-roofed canopy, with goodly pillars, the ceiling gorgeous with mosaics. Long colonnades, supported on 252 massive pillars, all richly carved and gilt, lead up to it. All day long circles of constantly renewed worshippers chant aloud the praises of Buddha, and the air is heavy with the effluvia of candles and the odours from thousands of smouldering incense sticks.

From consisting of wood, temples in Burma are liable to fire. The Incomparable Pagoda was thus destroyed in 1892.

CONCLUDING REMARKS ON HINDU TEMPLES.

Only a very few of the numberless Hindu Temples in India have been described. The great majority of them are small; but on some lakhs of rupees have been expended and a vast amount of labour. What are the results of all this outlay and toil?

1. **Loss of Money.**—By going to temples at a distance, people are taken away from their usual employments and cannot earn by them. They have also to incur travelling expenses. When worshippers arrive at their destination, they are beset by bloodsuckers who try to take from them every pice they can. The most outrageous lies are told to induce them to part with their money. To obtain what is required for a long pilgrimage, people sometimes contract debts which press heavily upon them the rest of their lives.

2. **Toil, Sickness, and Death.**—It is true that people can now go to many temples by railway; but generally they have still to walk many weary miles on foot, frequently in the hot season when it is most trying.

Great crowds sometimes assemble. The food is often unwholesome or badly cooked; supposed holy water from stagnant tanks is drunk for purification; the strength is sometimes reduced by want of sleep at night; the ground around is used for the calls of nature; the whole air becomes tainted with the most sickly smells. Not unfrequently cholera breaks out, and as the pilgrims separate they scatter the seeds of the disease in every direction. Thousands of people who stay at home lose their lives every year through cholera brought away by pilgrims.

Pilgrims are often attacked by sickness on the way; they lie down to die by the roadside, far away from any to comfort them in their last moments, and perhaps to be devoured by jackals. The principal lines of road to Puri may be traced by the skeletons along their sides.

3. **No Instruction is given on our duties to God or Man.**—A Hindu priest attached to a temple learns by heart and is able to repeat certain Sanskrit texts; but he never attempts to instruct the worshippers, for which, indeed, he is quite unfit. He can only mutter some words which the worshipper neither hears nor understands. The discharge of the above duties is never represented as enjoined by the gods, nor are any prayers offered to enable the worshippers to perform them aright.

4. **Increase of Wickedness.**—While no good advice is given, there is much to corrupt the worshippers. The managers of temples vie with each other in getting up entertainments to attract the masses. Crowds of prostitutes collect at great festivals to ply their trade. Some people go on pilgrimage, because they can indulge in acts of wickedness which they are afraid to do at home.

It is notorious that great places of pilgrimage are the wickedest cities in India. The chief occupation of the inhabitants is to cheat and plunder pilgrims.

Temples and cars are often ornamented with figures. Although unobjectionable for the most part, in some cases they are very obscene.

The Penal Code contains the following law against obscene books, pictures, and images:

"292. Whosoever sells or distributes, imports or prints for sale or hire, or wilfully exhibits to public view, any obscene book, pamphlet, paper, drawing, painting, representation, or figure, or attempts or offers so to do, shall be punished with imprisonment of either description for a term which may extend to three months, or with fine, or with both."

As Hindu temples often offend in the above respect, to prevent their prosecution, the following exemption had to be made:

"This Section does not extend to any representation sculptured, engraved, painted or otherwise represented on or in any temple or on any car used for the conveyance of idols, or kept or used for any religious purpose."

The sight of such objects must awaken impure feelings. That such an exception is necessary, is a terrible disgrace to Hinduism. There is probably no other religion now existing in the world requiring it. The most degraded savage does not so offend decency.

In not a few temples, the worshippers are also corrupted by dancing girls, professedly married to the gods, called *Deva Dasis*, but who are simply prostitutes.

Such women are the counterparts of the Apsaras in Indra's heaven. The Vishnu Purana and the Ramayana attribute their origin to the churning of the Ocean. When they came forth from the waters, neither the gods nor the Asuras would have done for wives, so they became common to all. They have the appellations of Surānganās, 'wives of the gods,' and Sumad-ātmajās, 'daughters of pleasure.'

5. **The Objects Worshipped give most degrading ideas of God.**—The most celebrated idol in India is that of Jagannath at Puri, of which a representation is given at page 4, and which is described by Dr. Rajendralala Mitra is a "most hideous caricature of the 'human face divine.'" But idolatry is to be condemned, however beautiful the image.

Hindus admit the Brahm is *nirákár*, without form. Christians say that God is a spirit. A sculptor may make an image of a man's body; but can he make a representation of his soul? It is equally impossible to make an idol like God. "To whom will ye liken me or shall I be equal?" saith the Holy One.

Various excuses are made for idolatry.

Some say that idols are only like photographs, recalling friends to memory. To this it has been well replied:

"It is true that we like to retain photographs of people we love to remind us of their forms and features; but of what sort of Divinity do blocks of stone or hideous images bought in the bazar remind us?"

If a son kept an image of a pig to remind him of his father, would this be right? would the father be pleased? It is infinitely worse to make an image of God.

But it is not true to say that idols are only to remind men of God. When a Hindu buys an idol or gets one made, he has the *pran pratishtha* ceremony performed, by which he believes that its nature is changed, and that it acquires not only life, but supernatural powers.

Statues of great men and women are often made for Europeans; but there is no *pran pratishtha* ceremony, nor are they worshipped.

Another excuse is that idolatry is allowable for the ignorant.

To this it is replied, how is it that every Muhammadan in Turkey and every Protestant Christian from the highest to the lowest, can worship God without images? The ignorant do not need images to remind them of God. They cannot understand His form, for He has none. They can remember their parents when far distant; they can love a benefactor whom they have never seen; they can obey the authority of a Queen-Empress though she never set foot on their soil. They can worship God who is a Spirit in spirit and in truth. Idols are a hindrance, not a help, to true worship. They give most degrading ideas of God. "The glory of the incorruptible God is changed into an image made like to corruptible man, and to birds, and fourfooted beasts, and creeping things."

6. **The mode of Worship is revolting.**—Details have been given of the religious services at famous temples. The very idea is horrible that men should pretend to awake God in the morning, and put Him to sleep as if He were a child, or that women should dance for His amusement as if He were a sensual Hindu Raja. At Bhuvaneswara, a block of granite is worshipped as a linga of the Swayambhu class. "The god's teeth are cleaned by

pouring water and rubbing a stick about a foot long on the stone." Does not this seem **awful** mockery?

7. **Worshippers are deceived by the most outrageous falsehoods.**—The following are some of the promises held out to pilgrims: It is said of a tree at Puri:—

"Whoever stands under the shadow of this tree, immediately clears himself from the sin of killing Brahmans. Of him who walks round the tree and then worships it, Hari remits all the sins committed in the course of a hundred generations."

A similar assertion is made of the Manikarnika well at Benares. All who die in that city, whatever crimes they have committed, are said to go to heaven.

Of the filthy tank at Bhuvaneswar in Orissa it is said:

"Whatever merits may be acquired by annual pilgrimages to the source of the Ganges, to Prayaga, or to Ganga Sagar, repeated for 60 years, may be acquired by a single bath in the Vindusagara and the adoration of Mahesvara." "The drinking of the water confers the dignity of Siva, and that dignity lasts as long as the sun."*

In Western India Brahmans claim that the Narbada is superior in sanctity to the Ganges; "One day's ablution in the Ganges frees from all sin; but the mere sight of the Narbada purifies from guilt. Furthermore, either bank of the Narbada may be used for burning the dead, whereas only the northern bank of the Ganges is effectual for that purpose."

At Kumbakonam in the Madras Presidency, it is asserted that every 12 years the waters of the Ganges flow underground into a certain tank, and multitudes bathe in it in the hope of washing away all their sins.

Like rival shopkeepers each declaring his goods to be the best in the world, so the different temples try to outvie with each other in telling the greatest lies about the merit to be acquired by visiting them, in order to extract money from simple-minded worshippers. Every intelligent Hindu must acknowledge that assertions like the above are pure falsehoods.

8. **Demerit, instead of Merit, is acquired by worshipping at such temples.**—There is a King renowned for his power, wisdom, and goodness. Some of his subjects, to whom he has shown great kindness, instead of acknowledging his authority, set up pretended kings of their own whom they honour and to whom they pay taxes instead of their rightful sovereign. Such persons are guilty of rebellion, the greatest crime in a state, and instead of being rewarded, they may expect to be severely punished.

Whom do the Hindus worship instead of the great Creator? Idols which can neither see nor hear; cows, monkeys, snakes; blocks of stone; the tools they use; anything except the great Being whom they ought to worship. God's first command is not to worship any other than Himself. The second is not to bow down to images. Hindus disobey both commands, and thus render themselves liable to the severest punishment.

9. **People are led to trust for salvation to refuges of lies.**—Purity of character is nothing; pilgrims are not told to be heartily sorry for their sins, to seek pardon from God, and ask His help to lead a new life. No: a man may live a life of the greatest villainy and be guilty of the most atrocious crimes, but let him eat of the *Mahaprasad* or bathe at certain places and all is well. The poor deluded victims are spending money for that which is not bread, and labour for that which satisfieth not. They leave the world with a lie in their right hand, saying, "peace, peace to themselves, when there is no peace." Only when it is too late will they find out the real state of things.

10. **The dishonesty often connected with temple management shows the worthlessness of Hinduism.**—To prevent fraud, Government formerly, to some extent, supervised the management of Hindu temples. There is a growing feeling in Europe that the care of religion should be left to its own professors, and not be undertaken by Government. On this principle Hindu Temples were handed over to the Hindus themselves. Everywhere there is a complaint of the maladministration of temple revenues, and the British Government has been petitioned to interfere again.

Christian and Hindu Worship Compared.

Hindu worship has already been described. Christian worship will now be noticed.

1. **The Building.**—This differs greatly in form from a Hindu temple. The object is to enable the people to worship together, and to receive instruction. There is therefore only one

* *Antiquities of Orissa*, Vol. II., p. 70.

building, varying in size and design according as it is situated in a village or in a city. Some can contain only a few worshippers: others can hold several thousands. In cities there are several churches.

There are no idols. One of the great commands of Christianity forbids the worship of images. It is true that Roman Catholic churches contain images; but these differ from Hindu idols, and many Christians object to them.

2. **Officers and Establishment.**—Except in some very large churches, the services are conducted by one person, set apart for the office. Such men should be selected with care for their piety, good conduct, and fitness. Afterwards they should have a training for some years to enable them to discharge aright their important duties.

Singing hymns forms a prominent part of Christian worship. Sometimes the music is led by an instrument, and there may be a band of singers, called a choir. The members of choirs, as a rule, are not paid, but belong to the congregation.

There is usually an officer who has charge of the building.

It need scarcely be mentioned that there are no *devadasis* connected with Christian Churches.

3. **The Service.**—Public worship among Christians consists in united prayer, the reading of the Bible, singing hymns, and a sermon or address. The form varies somewhat. To give a better idea of it, a short account will be given of the religious service at which the Queen-Empress of India is present every Sunday. First a verse of the Bible, like the following, is read:

"I will arise and go to my father, and will say unto him, Father, I have sinned against heaven, and before thee, and am no more worthy to be called thy son."

The people are then invited to confess their sins in the following words:—

"Almighty and most merciful Father, we have erred and strayed from Thy ways like lost sheep. We have followed too much the devices and desires of our own hearts. We have offended against Thy holy laws. We have left undone those things which we ought to have done; and we have done those things which we ought not to have done; and there is no health in us. But Thou, O Lord, have mercy upon us, miserable offenders. Spare Thou them, O God, which confess their faults. Restore Thou them that are penitent; according to Thy promises declared unto mankind in Christ Jesus our Lord. And grant, O most merciful Father, for his sake; that we may hereafter live a godly, righteous, and sober life, to the glory of Thy holy Name. *Amen.*"

One of the prayers used is called the "Lord's Prayer," because Jesus Christ taught it to His disciples:

"Our Father, which art in heaven, Hallowed be Thy name. Thy kingdom come. Thy will be done in earth, as it is in heaven. Give us this day our daily bread. And forgive us our trespasses as we forgive them that trespass against us. And lead us not into temptation; but deliver us from evil. For Thine is the kingdom, the power, and the glory, for ever. *Amen.*"

Portions from the Old and New Testaments are then read for the instruction of those present.

The singing of hymns is an important part of Christian worship. The following is a translation of one which has been used for nearly 3,000 years:

Before Jehovah's awful throne,
Ye nations, bow with sacred joy;
Know that the Lord is God alone;
He can create, and He destroy.

His sovereign power, without our aid,
Made us of clay, and formed us men;
And, when like wandering sheep we strayed,
He brought us to His fold again.

We are His people, we His care,—
Our souls and all our mortal frame:
What lasting honours shall we rear,
Almighty Maker, to Thy name?

We'll crowd Thy gates with thankful songs,
High as the heavens our voices raise;
And earth, with her ten thousand tongues,
Shall fill Thy courts with sounding praise.

Wide as the world is Thy command,
Vast as eternity Thy love;
Firm as a rock Thy truth must stand,
When rolling years shall cease to move.

A short statement of Christian belief, as follows, is repeated:

"I believe in God the Father Almighty, Maker of heaven and earth.

"And in Jesus Christ His only Son our Lord, who was conceived by the Holy Ghost, born of the Virgin Mary, suffered under Pontius Pilate, was crucified, dead and buried. He descended into hell (the unseen world); the third day He rose again from the dead, He ascended into heaven, and sitteth on the right hand of God the Father Almighty; from thence He shall come to judge the quick (living) and the dead.

"I believe in the Holy Ghost; the holy Catholic Church; the Communion of Saints; the Forgiveness of sins; the Resurrection of the body, and the life everlasting. *Amen.*"

In another part of the service, the Ten Commandments are repeated. The Minister stands up, and, in the name of God, enjoins the worshippers not to steal, not to bear false witness, not to commit adultery, not to commit any of the four offences against God or of the six offences against man forbidden in the Ten Commandments, and then after each proclamation of a commandment, he joins with the people in asking God to have mercy upon them, and to give them grace to keep that commandment better in future.

The Ten Commandments, in brief form, are as follows:

Duty to God.

1. Not to worship any other than the one true God.
2. Not to worship images.
3. Not to use God's name lightly.
4. To keep holy the Sabbath day.

Duty to Man.

5. Honor thy father and thy mother.
6. Thou shalt not kill.
7. Thou shalt not commit adultery.
8. Thou shalt not steal.
9. Thou shalt not bear false witness.
10. Thou shalt not covet.

The following thanksgiving is used towards the close of the service:—

"Almighty God, Father of all mercies, we Thine unworthy servants do give Thee most humble and hearty thanks for all Thy goodness and loving-kindness to us and to all men. We bless Thee for our creation, preservation, and all the blessings of this life; but above all, for Thine inestimable love in the redemption of the world by our Lord Jesus Christ; for the means of grace, and for the hope of glory. And, we beseech Thee, give us that due sense of all Thy mercies, that our hearts may be unfeignedly thankful, and that we show forth Thy praise, not only with our lips, but in our lives; by giving up ourselves to Thy service, and by walking before Thee in holiness and righteousness all our days; through Jesus Christ our Lord, to whom with Thee and the Holy Ghost be all honour and glory, world without end. *Amen.*"

Then follows a sermon, an address explaining some doctrine or enforcing some duty.

Contrast.—Hindu worship has been well compared to child's play. Little children talk to their dolls as if they had life. They dress them, pretend to give them food, put them to sleep, and so forth. Grown-up people do just the same. They treat their idols as living beings. They offer them food, though they cannot eat; they have different kinds of music before images that cannot hear; they have lights before what cannot see.

The very idea is horrible that men should pretend to awake God in the morning and put Him to sleep as if He were a child. The Omnipotent God fainteth not, neither is weary; He never slumbers nor sleeps.

No instruction on duties either to God or man is given in Hindu temples. The priest mutters some words in Sanskrit which the worshipper neither hears nor understands. He goes away grossly deceived, thinking that he has "seen God," and acquired a stock of merit, while he has only added to his sins.

Christian worship consists of prayer, the singing of hymns, the reading of the Scriptures, and addresses. These are intelligible to all, and fitted to have a very beneficial influence.

Compare also the *characters* of the objects of worship. Vishnu and Siva, the two principal Hindu gods, are represented in their own Puranas, as guilty of lying, theft, adultery, murder. The excuse is made for them that "The mighty are not to be blamed," the gods may act as they please. The reverse is the case. It would be a far greater crime for God to commit sin than for a man. There is a proverb *yathá devah tatha bhakthá*, 'As is the god so is the worshipper.' People tend to become like the objects of their worship. Vice is thus encouraged. On the other hand, the one true God worshipped in Christian Churches is spotlessly holy: sin is that abominable thing which He hates. *True* worshippers gradually become like Him.

But there are no such beings as Vishnu and Siva. They are the inventions of men who conceived gods after their own evil hearts. Let them no longer be worshipped; but let all, with deep sorrow for past sins, cast themselves at the feet of the one true God, the Creator and rightful Lord of the Universe, their Father in heaven, imploring forgiveness in the name of the Saviour, and striving, through the help of the Holy Spirit, to be His obedient and loving children in future.

APPEAL TO BUDDHISTS.

As has been quoted, "HINDUISM IS GOD WITHOUT MORALITY; BUDDHISM IS MORALITY WITHOUT GOD." Buddhism has been well described as a proud attempt to create a religion without God, and in which man is his own saviour. It is entirely silent about our duty to God. Christianity is "*God* WITH *morality*." Its *first* commend is LOVE TO GOD; its *second* LOVE TO MAN.

The following remarks are submitted to the consideration of thoughful Buddhists:

UNCERTAINTY ABOUT BUDDHA'S TEACHING.

Buddha did not write anything himself. The Sinhalese say that the three Pitakas were first reduced to writing at Aluwihara, near Mátalé, in the reign of Waligambahu I., 453 years after the death of Buddha.

Certain priests then wrote that they had heard from others, who heard from others, who heard from others, and so on, that Buddha had said or done certain things. What court of justice would accept such witness? Suppose a deed were executed in the name of a person 453 years after his death, what would be its value?

It is claimed that Rahats handed down correctly the words of Buddha, but of this there is no proof except the assertions of the priests. It will be shown that, whether correctly handed down or not, they contain gross errors.

The Pitakas were written by priests. The greater Buddha was made to appear, the more honour and gifts they expected for themselves. They claim to be living representatives of Buddha, and as such should not bow even to a king.

The Pitakas themselves show that Buddha was a mere man, subject to human infirmities. He required food and clothing; he became sick and had to take medicine; at last he grew old and weak, so that he compared himself to a worn-out cart; he took ill from eating pork, and died like any other man.

In the *Abhinishkramana Sutra* it is said that Raja Bimbisara asked Buddha, while he was yet living as an ascetic seeking for enlightenment, "Who or what are you? Are you a god, or a Naga, or Brahma, or Sakra, or a man, or a spirit?" Bodhisat answered truthfully, "Maharaja! I am no god or spirit, but a plain man seeking for rest, and so am practising the rules of an ascetic life."

The following remarks are on the supposition that the Pitakas truly represent Buddha's teaching:

BUDDHA'S CLAIM TO OMNISCIENCE.

Gautama rests his claim to be the greatest of beings mainly on his alleged omniscience. He was supposed to know all things, past, present, and to come. Hence he is called Buddha, the Enlightened One, *Sarvagnya,* the All-wise, and *Samma Sambuddha*, the Completely

Enlightened One. This knowledge, he asserted, was self-acquired, and not derived from any one. In the *Mahavagga* he says, "I am the all-knowing. By my own power I possess knowledge. Whom should I call my master? I have no teacher."

In a paper read by Mr. H. Dharmapala of Celyon at Chicago, the same assertion is made: "Infinite is the wisdom of the Buddha." (page 863.)

When a traveller tells wonderful tales about foreign lands, one way of testing his statements is to ascertain whether they are correct regarding a country with which we are ourselves acquainted.

Europeans have visited nearly every part of the world, and measured the distances of the different places. Hence they have been able to draw maps so correct that, guided by them, ships, sailing thousands of miles, arrive safely at their destination. The Buddhists of India sat in their houses, and described countries and worlds out of their own head. The people then, like children, pleased with wonderful tales, readily believed what was written. It is the same with ordinary Sinhalese and Burmese.

Buddha's Knowledge of Geography.—Buddha originally was a Hindu, and his ideas of geography and astronomy were those held by Hindus. According to Buddhism, there are countless worlds, called Sakwalas. In the centre of each there is a mountain called Maha Meru. In the *Saptasuryodgamana Sutraya*, Buddha says that Maha Meru is in length 84,000 yojanas,* in breadth, 84,000 yojanas, beneath the great sea 84,000 yojanas, and 84,000 yojanas above the sea. In the *Visuddhi Maggo* it is stated that Maha Meru is surrounded by seven circles of rocks, separated by seven seas. Outside the whole is the Sakwalagala, 1,203,450 yojanas in diameter. There are said to be fishes in the ocean 1,000 yojanas in size.

If an ant goes round an orange in the same direction, it comes to the place from which it started. In like manner, if people travel round the world in the same direction, they come at last to the place from which they set out. Thousands of travellers and sailors do this every year. The earth is known to be only about 8,000 miles in diameter. There is no space for a rock in it 84,000 yojanas in breadth. There is no such rock as Maha Meru; there are no rocky circles; there is no Sakwalagala; there are no fishes 1,000 yojanas in length.

Buddha's Explanation of Eclipses.—According to Buddhist books, the sun is 50 yojanas in diameter, and the moon 49 yojanas. Both are said to be inhabited by gods. The Asur Rahu is said to be 5,000 yojanas high, and to have a mouth 300 yojanas deep. Sometimes he covers the sun and moon with his hand, or hides them in his mouth.

Buddhists have what they call the *Chanda Pirit* and *Suriya Pirit*, to be repeated at eclipses of the moon and sun. The former is given as follows in the *Sanyutta Nikaya*:

"Thus I heard, Bhagava (Buddha) was living in Sawatthi, in the garden of Anatha Pindiko. At the time, the moon-god was seized by the Asur Rahu. Then the moon-god, remembering Buddha, spake this stanza:

> "Namó té Buddha wiratthu
> Wippamuttósi sabbadhi
> Sambádhipatipannosmi
> Tassa mé saranan' bhawáti."

"Adoration to thee, great Buddha! Thou art free from all impurities. I am distressed. Become thou a refuge to me." Then Bhagawá, in behalf of the moon-god, addressed Rahu thus:

"In the rahat Tathágato (Buddha) the moon-god has taken refuge. Rahu! Release thou the moon. The Buddhas are merciful to the world." Then the Asur Rahu, having released the moon-god, went in great haste to the place where the chief Asur, Wépachitti, was, and after approaching him stood in great terror on one side.

This is the *Chanda Pirit*. The *Suriya Pirit* is the same, substituting sun-god for moon-god, with this exception, that in speaking of the sun-god Buddha says:

"Rahu, swallow not the traveller through the skies, who, with the splendour of the heat of his shining orb, dissipates the darkness."

It is well known that eclipses of the moon are caused by the shadow of the earth falling upon it, and eclipses of the sun by the moon passing across it. Eclipses can be calculated

* The length of the yojana is uncertain. The Sinhalese regard it as about 16 miles in length; in India it is considered much less.

hundreds of years before they take place, and it can be told exactly how much of the sun or moon will be hidden. How could this be if eclipses were caused by an Asur?

Buddha's explanation of Earthquakes.—According to Buddhism, the earth of this world is 240,000 yojanas thick; under this is the Jala Polowa, the world of water, 480,000 yojanas in depth, and this is again supported by the Wá-Polowa, the world of wind, 960,000 yojanas in thickness.

Buddha, in the *Maha Parinibbána Suttanta*, gives the following account of the first way in which earthquakes originate:—

"The great earth rests on the world of water, and the water rests on the world of wind, and the wind rests on space. And at such times, Ananda, as the mighty winds blow, the waters are shaken by the mighty winds as they blow, and by the moving water the earth is shaken. These are the first cause of the appearance of a mighty earthquake."

The earth floats in the sky like the moon. There is no world of waters supporting it. If Buddha's explanation of earthquakes was correct, they would be felt at once over the whole earth, whereas they are generally confined to a small district.

Every well-educated man knows that Buddha's explanations of the above are entirely wrong, and disprove his claim to omniscience.

If Buddha's knowledge of this world was incorrect, the inference is that his religious teaching was equally erroneous.

Buddha's Grand Error.

A dish of curry and rice may be composed of good materials, but if some poison is mixed with it, it will cause the death of those by whom it is eaten. In like manner, though part of Buddha's teaching is good, there is mixed with it deadly error. At present only his grand error can be noticed.

Denial of a Creator.—Buddha did not expressly say that there is no Creator; but he implied it when he claimed to be the greatest being in the universe. It is also involved in his assertion that there is no eternal being.

A child should not only be kind and dutiful to his brothers and sisters, but love, honour and obey his parents. What would be thought of a teacher who taught the former but not the latter? Yet this is what Buddha has done. Among all his precepts there is not one about our duty to God, our heavenly Father, who first gave us life, and who preserves us in life every moment. We live upon His earth, and every thing we have comes from Him. This is a fatal defect. Buddha and his priesthood wished to obtain for themselves the respect which is due to God.

The need of a Creator may thus be shown:

Men do not exist by their own power. Who can say, "I made my own soul? I made my own body?" Can any one born of his mother say, "I made myself?" We therefore conclude that all men have been made, and that they live in consequence of the power of their Maker.

By whom were men made? Did their parents make them? Did their father and mother plan how the eyes should be made that the child might see? how the ears should be made that it might hear? &c. Nothing of the kind. The parents were only like the tools with which a skilful workman makes an image.

By whom, then, was the child made? It did not make itself; its parents did not make it. Did Buddha make it? Certainly not. He never said that he made the world or any of the men who lived in the world. Nor did he say that men were made by any of the gods.

It is objected that we owe our existence to *Karma*. People must have existed before they could have *Karma*. This is like saying that a cow was born from its own calf.

There must be a great Creator of the universe.

Effects of the Denial of a Creator in Buddhist Countries.

As a sky without a sun, so is a world without God—all is dark and miserable. When the existence of a great Creator and Ruler of the world is denied, men are very apt to give way to degrading superstitions. The Sinhalese and Burmese profess to take refuge in Buddha, his doctrines and his priesthood; but their real threefold refuge, are demon worship, astrology, and charms, although they are condemned in Buddhist books as "low arts and lying practices."

The ordinary Sinhalese Buddhist says: "Buddha is for the other world." He may go to the wihara once a month with offerings; he may join in a *pinkama*, he may put a little rice in the priest's bowl as he stands at the door; but his great concern is with the present. To use the words of Bishop Copleston: "The whole soil is covered with a thick and tangled growth of devil ritual, half Hindu and half savage, of charms, and sorcery, and astrology."

The last census showed that there were 2,043 devil-dancers in the Island, one-half of them in the Southern Province, the stronghold of Buddhism. Under devil-dancing may be included the whole class of idolatrous and superstitious rites, incantations and invocations. The Sinhalese Buddhists serve not only *yakun* or demons, but some of the Hindu deities, as Indra and Vishnu, many local gods, and the supposed powers which haunt trees, and jungles and ponds.

Every child has his horoscope written; lucky and unlucky days are observed; protection threads are tied on the arm; charms are written and placed in cases on the person; images are made with the stabbing or destruction of which the object of the believer's spite is to perish; there are preparations to bring specified calamities on the person who passes under or over or near them. Whatever form of sorcery one has anywhere read of, is found in operation in Ceylon. Of omens which determine the luck or ill-luck of an enterprise, or oblige the traveller to abandon his journey, the list would be endless. The Buddhist moves in a world haunted and beset by the supernatural, breathing an atmosphere heavy with fears and suspicions.*

In this dependence on supposed powers which have no relation to good and bad and which make no claim to reverence, there is nothing likely to form a keen sense of right and wrong. Some of the charms are truly horrible; as "eat his flesh and drink his blood." There is no demon to fulfil such a request; but it makes him who utters it bring down a curse upon his own head.

The same demon worship and other superstitions prevail in Burma. Buddhists are kept in constant terror of beings which have no more existence than the goblins with which ignorant parents frighten children.

NO SALVATION BY BUDDHISM.

"What must I do to be saved from hell and rise to heaven?" is the most important question which we can ask. Our everlasting happiness depends upon its correct answer. This paper is intended to assist in the search.

1. **Buddhism has no pardon of Sin.**—None can deny that they are sinful. Most people, it is true, have only very faint ideas of their guilt. Those who reflect seriously have a very different opinion. They know that thoughts may be sinful as well as words and actions; that we may sin both in what we leave undone as well as in what we do. They feel that not a day of their life passes in which many sins are not committed. A good man of old said, "My sins are more than the hairs of my head." According to *karma* every sin must be punished: the *phala* (fruit) of every action must be eaten. The Dhamma-pada says, "Not in the heavens, O man, not in the midst of the sea, not if thou hidest thyself in the clefts of the mountains, wilt thou find a place where thou canst escape the force of thine own evil actions." According to Buddhism, man is bound hand and foot to the inevitable consequences of his own evil deeds.

Buddha could not pardon sin or save men from its consequences. Buddhaghosa mentions that certain disciples of Buddha, although they had reached the state of holy men, yet, on account of a sin formerly committed, fought among themselves, and all killed each other, while Buddha had no power to prevent their suffering the punishment of this sin. When the flames of the Awichi hell enwrapped the body of Dewadatta, he besought Buddha to save him on account of his relationship; but Buddha said that not ten, nor a hundred, nor even a thousand Buddhas could deliver him.

According to Buddhism, there are eight principal *narakas*, or places of punishment, in

* Abridged from Bishop Copleston's Paper on Buddhism.

all 136. Even in the first hell, those who go there are said to be confined 160,000 kelas of the years of men. What a fearful prospect to a dying Buddhist!

Buddha never claimed to set men free from the penalty of sin. On the contrary, he taught that punishment follows sin as the wheel follows the ox.

2. **Buddhism gives no help in walking in the right way.**—As it has no pardon for past sins, so it gives no aid in guarding against them in future.

The Eightfold Path enjoins Right Thought, Right Speech, Right Actions, &c. How are we to be able to walk in it? We are in ourselves weak, inclined to evil, averse to what is good. Long ago a poet sorrowfully said, "I see and approve of what is right; but I do what is wrong." We need strength to resist temptation and to do our duty.

Buddhists now say, *Buddhan saranan gachami,* "I make Buddha my refuge; but they also admit that Buddha has obtained *nirwana* that he no longer exists; that he cannot hear them when they cry to him. Buddha, shortly before his death, said to his followers, *attasaraná viharatha,* "Be your own refuge." Man is not to look for help to any other than himself, he is to be his own saviour, his own god.

As a little child, without the help of his father's hand, is unable to walk along a rough and stony road, so we need divine help to walk in the path of holiness. Buddhism leaves man to himself: it has no prayer for help.

3. **Buddhism has no permanent happiness, and, in the end, leads to everlasting death.**

What is the prospect until *nirwana* is obtained?

Prince Mahanama thus describes to his brother Anuradha the alternate happiness and misery of life:—

"The being who is still subject to birth may at one time sport in the beautiful garden of a deva-loka, and at another be cut to a thousand pieces in hell; at one time he may be Maha Brahma, and at another a degraded outcaste; at one time he may eat the food of the devas, and at another he may have molten lead poured down his throat; at one time he may sip nectar, and at another he may be made to drink blood."

What is the final reward after enduring all such terrible suffering? NIRVANA.

Life is compared to the flame of a lamp. A flame blown out has no existence; so a person who has entered *Nirvana* ceases to exist. Buddhism puts an end to the man's sufferings by putting an end to his life.

It will be seen from the foregoing remarks that Buddhism has no pardon of past sins, no help to avoid them in time to come, no permanent happiness. It may, therefore, justly be said to have no salvation; it only professes to point out the road to eternal death, to the destruction of suffering by the destruction of being.

Is there any religion by which man's three great wants can be supplied? Yes, there is one which meets them all.

1. **Christianity shows how pardon of sin may be obtained.**—Buddha denied the existence of an eternal Creator, and tried to place *karma* in His stead. In the *Cullakamma-wibhanga Sutra*, Buddha says, "*Karma* divides to beings prosperity or adversity." Consideration will show that this is impossible.

A judge of the Supreme Court requires great knowledge, wisdom, and justice. To ascribe such qualities to a mere word is folly: an intelligent living being is required. If instead of *karma* we read God, all is plain.

While prayer cannot be addressed to *karma*, while it cannot remit the penalty, it is different with God. A king has power to pardon the offences of his subjects, so God has power to forgive sin. Our hearts teach us to pray.

God is our Father in heaven. He gave us life; He supports us in life. We live in the world which He created. Though we have been disobedient, rebellious children, He yearns over us with a father's love, and is not willing that we should perish. But He is also our King, and His laws must not be broken with impunity. In His great love, He devised a way in which justice and mercy may both be satisfied. God gave His only Son to be our Saviour. Becoming man, He was born as the Lord Jesus Christ. After leading a perfectly holy life, He died on the cross for man's salvation. On the third day He rose from the dead, and afterwards ascended to heaven. Pardon is now freely offered to all who trust in Jesus Christ as their Saviour, and seek it in His name. Say, "O God, my Heavenly Father, I have sinned against Thee. I take refuge in Thy Son; for His sake forgive all my sins."

2. **Christianity gives us help in leading a holy life.**—We need more than pardon. It is *sin* which is the cause of suffering, and to be freed from suffering we must be freed from sin. We are as unfit to enter heaven as filthy lepers would be to go into a king's palace.

We are so "tied and bound with the chains of our sins" that deliverance is impossible without Divine help. This is freely offered. The Holy Spirit is able and willing to help us. Say, "O eternal God, my heavenly Father, for the sake of Thy Son, give me Thy Holy Spirit to cleanse my heart from all sin." At the same time, we must watch against temptation, and use all the means provided for our growth in holiness.

3. **Christianity offers us everlasting happiness.**—In this world we are like sick persons, requiring sometimes to take unpleasant medicines. Christians, however, are comforted amid all the trials of life, knowing that they are under the watchful care of their heavenly Father, that "all things work together for good to them that love God."

The only thing we know about ourselves with certainty is that we must die. The mightiest king cannot resist the stroke of death. Compare the feelings of a dying Buddhist and a dying true Christian.

The Buddhist does not know what will befal him. If he thinks seriously he must know that he has committed many sins in this life, and there may be innumerable others in former births requiring him to endure excruciating punishment for kelas of years. Well may he exclaim, like a dying man in old times, "In great alarm I depart."

How different are the feelings of a true Christian when dying! Death is not an executioner about to drag him to an *awichi* hell; but a messenger calling him to dwell for ever in his Father's palace. His sins have been forgiven through Jesus Christ. He does not hope to get to heaven through his own merits; but on account of the spotless righteousness of Jesus Christ. Jesus Christ said to the dying thief on the cross, "To-day shalt thou be with me in paradise." The Christian, at death, passes at once into joy unspeakable. His heaven is not happiness for a time and then misery; but pleasures for evermore, and always increasing.

Buddha says, "All things are unabiding." This is not true. There is an eternal God, without beginning and without end. Instead of seeking refuge in a dead, annihilated man or in yourself, make the eternal God your refuge, through the Lord Jesus Christ.

Buddhism is the path to everlasting death; Christianity the path to everlasting life: which will you choose?

The Two First Sermons.

The following extract from Buddha's First Sermon contains the substance of his doctrine:

"Birth is suffering. Decay is suffering. Illness is suffering. Death is suffering. Presence of objects we hate is suffering. Separation from objects we love is suffering. Not to obtain what we desire is suffering. Clinging to existence is suffering. Complete cessation of thirst, or of craving for existence, is cessation of suffering; and the eightfold path which leads to cessation of suffering is right belief, right aspiration, right speech, right conduct, right means of livelihood, right endeavour, right memory, right meditation. This is the noble truth of suffering."

Extract from the First Sermon of Jesus Christ:

"The Spirit of the Lord is upon Me, because He hath anointed Me to preach good tidings to the poor; He hath sent Me to heal the broken-hearted, to preach deliverance to the captives, and recovering of sight to the blind, to set at liberty them that are bruised, to preach the acceptable year of the Lord."

What is there of hope for poor suffering humanity in the first utterance of the Buddha? It is the gospel of despair; while the other message is a proclamation of good tidings of great joy to all people.

The Two Physicians.

A man is sick and suffering pain. A physician is called in. He says the sick man will suffer as long as he lives. He therefore recommends a large dose of opium, which will put an end to his sufferings by putting an end to his life.

RUINS OF THE TEMPLE OF NEPTUNE.

Another physician offers his help. Instead of saying that the disease is incurable and giving a dose of opium, he, at great sacrifice to himself, provides a medicine which restores the sick man to perfect health.

The first physician is Buddha. He says that " existence is suffering." His path to the destruction of suffering is by the destruction of being.

The second physician is Jesus Christ. He says that to the man who lives rightly, "existence is happiness." He destroys suffering by the destruction of sin, and offers us everlasting happiness in heaven.

Which of these physicians will you choose ?

THE FUTURE OF HINDU TEMPLES.

It is a trite saying that " History repeats itself." Christianity is now seeking to become the religion of India, as it sought, 18 centuries ago, to become the religion of Europe. The circumstances are very much alike, and so will be the final result.

It is well known that the ancestors of the Eastern and Western Aryans once lived together, speaking the same language, and worshipping the same gods. Even after the latter went to Europe, they agreed in many things. They had their schools of philosophy like the Hindus ; their gods were said to have behaved much in the same way as those of India, and were worshipped with similar rites.

It is remarkable in how many respects India, at present, resembles Europe when the Gospel was first brought to its shores.

A single Government, like the Roman Empire, prevented national wars which would have rendered impossible the free and frequent passage of missionaries from country to country. The world-wide feeling thus awakened was some preparation for the universal spiritual kingdom which was sought to be established. The Roman highways were travelled by Christian preachers, and an Alexandrian ship, bound to Rome with corn, afforded a passage to the Apostle Paul. The Greek tongue was known, more or less, in all the countries washed by the Mediterranean.

The Roman Emperors had no wish to promote the spread of Christianity. Till the time of Constantine, they rather exerted their power to check its progress. The British Government, without intending it, is similarly preparing the way for the Gospel in India. Formerly the country was divided into numerous states, frequently at war with one another, preventing free communication. Now all can travel, without hindrance, from the Himalayas to Cape Comorin. Roads, railways and steam-vessels afford facilities for moving about, never possessed before. The English language is tending powerfully to weld together educated men of different nationalities. India is the great seat of caste, which splits up its races into small sections, regarding each other with mutual jealousy. Ideas of the " Brotherhood of Man " are gradually being diffused, hastening on the time when all shall be one body in Christ.

Attempts to reform Hinduism.—Philosophers and the Emperor Julian in ancient Europe attempted to reform the heathenism of their time by copying some of the features of Christianity. Similar efforts are now being made by some in India to frame a new Hinduism, which will bear the fierce light of the nineteenth century.

A Bengali novelist tried to whitewash Krishna, holding him up as the embodiment of all virtue. Swami Vivekananda, at the Chicago " Parliament of Religions," was discreetly silent regarding certain Hindu doctrines and practices, while he attempted to palm off as Hindu what he had learned as a student in a Christian college. " The Fatherhood of God and the Brotherhood of Man" are now claimed by some as the teaching of Hinduism. Christian forms of worship have been adopted by the Brahmos, and lately in Madras a *Hindu* Young Men's Association has been established on a Christian Model.

Ancient Temples in Europe allowed to become ruins or converted into churches.—Eighteen centuries ago, the whole Roman Empire was studded with the temples of Jupiter and Juno, Apollo and Minerva, Neptune, Mars and other supposed deities. As Christianity spread, the temples were gradually deserted. The Emperor Julian found at Antioch a famous temple of Apollo in ruins. It was restored with the greatest splendour. Julius went there to offer a sacrifice to the god. He expected to find a multitude of worshippers; but no one brought oil for a lamp or incense to burn in honour of the deity. Only an old man appeared to sacrifice a goose. The attempted revival of heathenism in Europe ended in failure.

The picture on page 94 shows the ruins of a temple of Neptune, god of the sea. There is not now a single worshipper of Jupiter, or Neptune, or of the great goddess Diana whose image is said to have fallen down from heaven. Some of the temples were converted into churches, but many were allowed to fall into decay. Only the ruins of a few remain till the present day. So will it yet be in India. The temples of Vishnu and Siva will be as deserted as those of Jupiter and Diana. "The gods that have not made the heaven and the earth, even they shall perish from the earth and under those heavens." The Eastern and Western Aryans will yet kneel at the same footstool, and offer the same grand old prayer, beginning, "Our Father which art in heaven."

ENGLISH PUBLICATIONS FOR INDIAN READERS.

RELIGIOUS REFORM.

THE SACRED BOOKS OF THE EAST DESCRIBED AND EXAMINED.

Attention is invited to the following volumes of the Series, now available:

AN ACCOUNT OF THE VEDAS, WITH ILLUSTRATIVE EXTRACTS FROM THE RIG-VEDA. 8vo. 166 pp. 4½ As. Post-free, 6 As.

The principal divisions of the Vedas are described; with life in Vedic times, the gods of the Vedas, the offerings and sacrifices. Through the kind permission of Mr. R. T. B. Griffith, translations of some of the most important hymns in the Rig-Veda are quoted in full.

THE ATHARVA-VEDA. 8vo. 76 pp. 2½ As. Post-free, 3 As.

A classified selection of the Hymns is given, including charms to cure diseases, expel demons, secure success in life, destroy enemies, &c., with a Review of the whole.

THE BRAHMANAS OF THE VEDAS. 8vo. 232 pp. BY THE REV. K. S. MACDONALD, M.A., D.D., Author of *The Vedic Religion.* 8 As. Post-free, 10 As. Half cloth, 12 As.

Accounts are given of the Brahmanas of the Rig-Veda, Sama Veda, Black and White Yajur Vedas, and the Atharva Veda, showing the development of Hinduism. The state of Society, the Human, Horse, and other Sacrifices, the Gods and Religion of the Brahmanas are described, with many interesting details.

SELECTIONS FROM THE UPANISHADS. 8vo. 120 pp. 4 As. Post-free, 5 As.

The Katha, Isa, and Svetásvatara, as translated into English by Dr. Roer, are quoted in full, with the notes of Sankara Achárya and others; and there are copious extracts from the Brihad Aranya and Chhándogya Upanishads; with an examination of their teaching.

STUDIES IN THE UPANISHADS. 8vo. 80 pp. 2½ As. Post-free, 3 As.

Five Lectures by the Rev. T. E. Slater. An interesting account is given of the development of ancient Indian thought, and its practical results in the life and the religion of the people. The Vedánta is contrasted with Christianity.

THE BHAGAVAD GITA. 8vo. 108 pp. 4 As. Post-free, 5 As.

An English translation carefully revised; numerous Explanatory Notes, and an Examination of its Doctrines.

THE VEDANTA-SARA. 8vo. 143 pp. 4 As. Post-free, 5½ As.

An English translation, by the late Dr. Ballantyne, Principal of the Sanskrit College, Benares, of the celebrated treatise of Sadánanda, with an introductory sketch of Hindu Philosophy, and brief summary of the Vedánta-Sútras. and an examination of the system. The proofs were read by Col. G. A. Jacob, Author of *Hindu Pantheism* and of a *Concordance to the Upanishads.*

THE VISHNU PURANA. 8vo. 96 pp. 3 As. Post-free, 4 As.

An abridgment is given, *verbatim*, from the English translation of H. H. Wilson, Professor of Sanskrit, University of Oxford; with an examination of the Book in the light of the present day.

THE RAMAYANA. 8vo. 180 pp. 7 As. Post-free, 8½ As. Half cloth, 11 As.

A full abridgment of this celebrated poem is given in English, with explanatory notes, where necessary. An Introduction treats of the author and age of the poem, with explanations of its aims by eminent Oriental scholars; it is compared with the Mahábhárata and the Greek epic poems. The review describes the state of society during the times of the author; the claims of the poem to be a sacred book are examined; and, in conclusion, an account is given of the Nishkalank or Spotless Avatár.

YOGA SASTRA. 8vo. 78 pp. 2½ As. Post-free, 3 As.

The Yoga Sútras of Patanjali examined, and the supposed Yoga powers shown to be a delusion. The true Yoga Sastra is explained; with a notice of Swami Vivekananda's Yoga Philosophy.

SELECTIONS FROM THE KORAN. 8vo. 232 pp. 8 As. Post-free, 10 As. Half cloth, 12 As.

Upwards of five hundred of the most important passages are given, with headings, explanatory Notes where necessary, and a classified Index. An introduction treats of the Koran, its Divisions, Sources, &c.; the Creed, Duties, Sects and Feasts of Islam. The Review shows the testimony of the Koran to the Christian Scriptures; its claim to inspiration is examined; with an address to enlightened Muslims. Throughout, extracts are given from standard works on the subject.

Miscellaneous.

A Rational Refutation of the Hindu Philosophical Systems. 2nd Edition. 8vo. 208 pp. Price 10 As. net, Post-free.

By Nehemiah Nilakantha Sâstri Goreh. Translated from the original Hindi, printed and manuscript, by Fitz-Edward Hall, D.C.L., *Oxon.*, H. M.'s Inspector of Public Instruction for the Central Provinces.

History of the Hindu Triad. (Brahma, Vishnu, and Siva) 8vo. 64 pp. 2 As. Post-free, 2½ As.

An account is first given of the earliest gods of the Hindus; the changes which afterwards took place are described; with the development of the Triad as given in the Hindu sacred books.

Popular Hinduism, 8vo. 96 pp. 2½ As. Post-free, 3½ As.

Review of the Hinduism of the Epic Poems and Puranas, &c.; Rites and Observances; Effects of Hinduism, and Suggested Reforms.

Philosophic Hinduism. 8vo. 72 pp. 2½ As. Post-free, 3 As.

The Upanishads; the Six Schools of Hindu Philosophy; the Minor Schools; Doctrines of Philosophic Hinduism; the Bhagavad Gita; Causes of the Failure of Hindu Philosophy.

The Brahma Samaj, and other Modern Eclectic Religious Systems. 108 pp. 3 As. Post-free, 4 As.

Modern Hindu Theism; Ramohun Roy; Debendranath Tagore; Keshub Chunder Sen; Sadharan Brahmo Samaj; Madras Brahmoism; Prarthana Samajes.

India Hindu, and India Christian; or, What Hinduism has done for India, and what Christianity would do for it. 8vo. 72 pp. 2½ As. Post-free, 3 As.

Address to thoughtful Hindus, showing how much their country would benefit from the religion which many of them now oppose.

Krishna as described in the Puranas and Bhagavad Gita. 8vo. 72 pp. 2½ As. Post-free, 3 As.

A full account is given of the Krishna Avatára, chiefly taken from the Vishnu Purana, with some extracts from the Bhagavata Purana and the Mahábhárata; the circumstances which led to the great war between the Pandus and Kurus are described; and some of the doctrines of the Bhagavad Gita are examined in detail.

Account of the Temple of Jagannath at Puri. 8vo. 48 pp. 1½ As.

The account is taken chiefly from Dr. Rajendralala Mitra's *Antiquities of Orissa*; Hunter's *Gazetteer of India*, Sterling's *Orissa*, &c. With views of the temple, procession, and images.

Christianity Explained to a Hindu; or, The Doctrines of Christianity and Hinduism Compared. 60 pp. 2 As.

Doctrines about God, Creation, the Soul, Karma, Transmigration, Sin, Incarnations, Salvation, Prospects at Death, and Comparative Effects.

Swami Vivekananda on Hinduism. 8vo. 96 pp. 3 As. Post-free, 4 As.

The Swami's Chicago Address is quoted in full and examined; important facts are brought out which he omitted to state.

Swami Vivekananda and his Guru. 8vo. 125 pp. 3 As. Post-free, 4 As.

A history of the Swami and his Guru is given; the Swami's boasted success in the West is shown to be untrue by the letters of 45 prominent Americans; the Vedánta philosophy is examined; portraits are given of Schopenhauer and Max Müller, with an estimate of the importance to be attached to their approval of Vedántism.

The History of Christianity in India; with its Prospects. 8vo. 150 pp. 5 As. Post-free, 6 As.

An account of the early Christian Missions, and the progress of Christianity among the principal nations; with 35 illustrations, including portraits of some eminent Missionaries.

Testimonies of Great Men to the Bible and Christianity. 8vo. 45 pp. 1½ As. Post-free, 2 As.

Opinions expressed by great writers, philosophers, scientists, lawyers and statesmen, showing that the Bible and Christianity are firmly believed by the most eminent men of the time.

How the People of Ancient Europe became Christians, and the Future Religion of India. 8vo. 48 pp. 1½ As. Post-free, 2 As.

An account of the Eastern and Western Aryans; their common origin; resemblances in language and religion; how Christianity was first brought to Europe; the opposition it encountered, and its final success, with the evidence that it will follow a similar course in India.

Civilization, Ancient and Modern, Compared; with Remarks on the study of Sanskrit. 8vo. 48 pp. 1½ As. Post-free, 2 As.

Devil-Dancers, Witch-Finders, Rain-Makers, and Medicine Men. 4to. 60 pp. 2½ As. Post-free, 3 As.

A full account of these curious and degrading superstitions, prevalent among backward nations in different parts of the world; with 36 illustrations.

Transmigration. 12mo. 19 pp. By Rev. Dr. W. Hooper, 1 Anna.

Doddridge's Rise and Progress of Religion in The Soul. 12mo. 180 pp. 3 As. Post-free, 4 As.

This is an abridged edition of one of the most useful works on Christianity in the English language.

Barrows Lectures. First Series. 8vo. 188 pp. 6 As.

Seven Lectures, by the Rev. Dr. J. H. Barrows, on Christianity, the World-Wide Religion.

Short Papers for Seekers after Truth. 12mo. 112 pp. 1 Anna.

A Guide to Religious Inquirers, treating of the Existence of God, Sin, the Need of a Revelation, the leading Doctrines of Christianity, and the Object of Life.

Short Papers for Young Men. 12mo. 104 pp. 1 Anna.

A Sequel to the foregoing. Hints on General Conduct, the Choice of a Profession, and Success in Life.

SOCIAL REFORM.

On Decision of Character and Moral Courage. 8vo. 56 pp. 1½ As. Post-free, 2 As.

A reprint of Foster's Celebrated Essay, with some remarks on its application to India.

Sanitary Reform in India. 68 pp. 2 As. Post-free, 2½ As.

How lakhs of Lives may be saved every year, and crores of cases of Sickness prevented; Precautions against Fever, Cholera, Diabetes, &c.

Is India becoming Poorer or Richer? With Remedies for the Existing Poverty. 8vo. 82 pp. 2½ As. Post-free, 3 As.

The prevailing idea with regard to the increasing poverty of India shown to be incorrect, and the true means of promoting its wealth explained.

Debt and the Right Use of Money. 8vo. 32 pp. 1 Anna.

Prevalence of Debt in India; its Causes; Evils; how to get out of it; with Franklin's Way to Health, &c.

Purity Reform. 8vo. 32 pp. 1 Anna.

The great need of this reform shown, and the means for its promotion.

Temperance Reform in India. 8vo. 40 pp. 1½ As. Post-free, 2 As.

Intoxicating liquors in Ancient India; Intemperance in England; Temperance Reform in the West; spread of Intemperance in India; Temperance Reform in India; how to promote Temperance Reform; with Portraits of Livesey, Father Mathew. Sir Wilfred Lawson, Dean Farrar, Messrs. Samuel Smith and Caine.

Caste. 8vo. 66 pp. 2 As. Post-free, 2½ As.

Supposed and real origin of Caste; Laws of Caste according to Manu; its Effects; Duty with regard to it.

The Women of India and What can be Done for Them. 8vo. 158 pp. 4 As. Post-free, 5½ As.

Women in Hindu literature; Female Education; Marriage Customs; Widow Marriage; means to be adopted to raise the position of Women.

The above complete in one volume, 1 Rupee Net. Postage, 2½ As.

Prize Essay on the Promotion of Indian Domestic Reform. 8vo. 144 pp. 4 As. Post-free, 5 As.

The prize was gained by Ganpat Lakshman, of Bombay, in 1841. His Essay was published with a Prefatory Note by the Rev. Dr. John Wilson, in which it is highly commended as giving a graphic and correct picture of Hindu family life.

Biographies.

Statesmen of Recent Times. 8vo. 192 pp. 8 As. Post-free, 9½ As.

Accounts are given of the leading Statesmen in the great countries of the world; as Gladstone, Salisbury, Bismarck, and others. Special notice is taken of those interested in India. In all 182 are mentioned, with 122 portraits.

The Governors-General of India, First Series. By Henry Morris, M. C. S. (retired) 8vo. 145 pp. 4 As. Post-free, 5 As.

Contains sketches of the lives of Warren Hastings, Lord Cornwallis, Sir John Shore, Marquis Wellesley, the Earl of Minto, and the Marquis of Hastings, with portraits. Interesting personal details are given, such as are not usually found in histories.

The Governors-General of India, Second Series. By the same author, 8vo. 175 pp. 4 As. Post-free 5 As.

Includes sketches of Lord Amherst, Lord William Bentinck, Lord Auckland, Lord Ellenborough, Lord Hardinge, and the Marquis of Dalhousie.

The two Series, half bound in cloth, gilt title, 12 As.

SKETCHES OF INDIAN CHRISTIANS; WITH AN INTRODUCTION BY S. SATTHIANADHAN, M.A. 8vo. 268 pp. half cloth with gilt title, 10 As. Post-free, 11½ As.

An account of 42 Indian Protestant Christians; Tamil, Telugu, Canarese, Malayalam, Bengali, Hindustani, Punjabi, Afghan, Gujarati, Marathi, Parsi, and Karen; with several portraits.

ANGLO-INDIAN WORTHIES. By Henry Morris, MADRAS C. S. (Retired.) 8vo. 160 pp. 4 As. Post-free, 5 As. Full cloth; gilt title, 8 As.

Lives of Sir Thomas Munro, Sir John Malcolm, Lord Metcalfe, Mountstuart Elphinstone, James Thomason, Sir Henry Lawrence, Sir James Outram, Sir Donald Macleod, and Sir Bartle Frere, with portraits.

EMINENT FRIENDS OF MAN; OR LIVES OF DISTINGUISHED PHILANTHROPISTS. 8vo. 158 pp. 4 As. Post-free, 5 As. Full cloth, gilt title, 10 As.

Sketches of Howard, Oberlin, Granville Sharp, Clarkson, Wilberforce, Buxton, Pounds, Davies of Devauden, George Moore, Montefiore, Livesey, the Earl of Shaftesbury, and others; with remarks on what might be done in India.

SOME NOTED INDIANS OF MODERN TIMES. 8vo. 164 pp. 4 As. Post-free, 5 As.

Sketches of Indian Religious and Social Reformers, Philanthropists, Scholars, Statesmen, Judges, Journalists, and others; with several portraits.

MARTIN LUTHER, THE GREAT EUROPEAN REFORMER. 8vo. 109 pp. 2½ As. Post-Free, 3 As.

The state of religion in Europe in the time of Luther is described; a full account is given of his undaunted efforts to bring about a reformation; the greater need of a similar change in India is shown, and Luther is held up as an example. 15 illustrations.

BABA PADMANJI. An Autobiography. 8vo. 108 pp. 2½ As. Post-free, 3 As.

An interesting account by himself of this popular Marathi author, describing his conversion from Hinduism to Christianity.

PICTURE STORIES OF NOBLE WOMEN. 4to. 50 pp. 2½ As. Post-free, 3 As.

Accounts of Cornelia, Agrippina, Padmani of Chittore, Lady Jane Grey, Ahaliya Bai, Mrs. Fry, Princess Alice, Miss Carpenter, Maharani Surnomayi, Pandita Ramabai, Miss Nightingale, and Lady Dufferin.

THE QUEEN-EMPRESS OF INDIA AND HER FAMILY. 43 pp. 3 As. Post-free, 3½ As.

Her early life; marriage; widowhood; children; progress in India during her reign; traits of character and lessons from her life. With 27 illustrations, and coloured portrait of the Empress.

SIR HERBERT EDWARDES. By Henry Morris. 8vo. 20 pp. ½ Anna.

He is described as the hero of Multan; the peacemaker among wild Afghan tribes; the true friend of India; the earnest Christian.

CHARLES GRANT: the Christian Director of the East India Company. By Henry Morris. 8vo. 48 pp. 1 Anna.

Mr. Grant was an esteemed Indian Civilian, who, after his retirement, became a Director and Chairman for a time of the East India Company. Some very important beneficial changes introduced by him are described. With a portrait.

JOHN CHRYSOSTOM: "THE GOLDEN-MOUTHED." 4to. 52 pp. 2 As.

An account of the most eloquent Christian preacher in ancient times; with a description of the age in which he lived, and the sufferings he endured. Illustrated by engravings.

Progress.

This is a monthly illustrated Periodical for the educated classes in India and Ceylon. The subscription is only 8 As. a year; with postage 14 As. Three copies may be sent for ½ anna postage.

The Periodical is specially recommended to TEACHERS. It would give new ideas to their pupils, while the page for students would be very useful to those preparing for examinations. Orders to be addressed to MR. A. T. SCOTT.

Orders to be addressed to MR. A. T. SCOTT, Tract Depôt, MADRAS, or to the Calcutta, Allahabad, Lahore, Simla, Bombay, Bangalore and Colombo Book Depôts.